Your
Forgotten
Self

DAVID ROBERT ORD

Your
Forgotten
Self

—

MIRRORED IN
JESUS THE CHRIST

NAMASTE PUBLISHING
Vancouver, Canada

Library and Archives Canada Cataloguing in Publication

Ord, David Robert _Your forgotten self : as mirrored in Jesus the Christ /
David Robert Ord.

Includes bibliographical references. _ISBN 978-1-897238-33-2

1. Jesus Christ—Example. 2. Jesus Christ—Character.
3. Self-realization—Religious aspects—Christianity. 4. Christian life.
I. Title.
BV4509.5.O73 2007   232.9'03   C2007-902657-5

Published by Namaste Publishing
P.O. Box 62084
Vancouver, BC, Canada V6J 4A3
www.namastepublishing.com
namaste@telus.net

Distributed in North America by Hampton Roads Publishing Company
Charlottesville, VA, USA
hrpc@hrpub.com

Printed and bound in Canada by Friesens Printing

To my son Julian who has always believed in my writing,
to Lucinda for all the support she has given me
in writing this particular book,
to Sebastian without whom this book
would never have happened, and
to Constance who had the faith to publish it.

Contents

Note About the Use of Language and Biblical Translation

Throughout this work, I have endeavored to avoid non-inclusive language. Because the repeated use of she/he, and so forth, seems cumbersome, I have opted for the simpler use of the plurals "they," "them" and "their."

For the sake of familiarity, I have chosen to use the New King James Version of the Bible, except where otherwise noted. Unfortunately, this translation renders the Hebrew and Greek texts in non-inclusive language.

For readers seeking a thorough biblical grounding of the book's content, a section of endnotes is provided as background.

Acknowledgments

It was in 1990 that I was first introduced to the insights of Sebastian Moore, a British Monk at Downside Abbey near Bath. Subsequently, we began a lengthy correspondence, and I eventually traveled to the abbey to meet him.

Though Sebastian has published some of his insights, his work is now mostly out of print. Much of what I learned from him came not from his published work but from his prolific correspondence with me, beginning in 1991 and continuing up until the present.

Sebastian's insights into the nature of God and Jesus so dovetailed with my own understanding, and were so refreshingly different from traditional Christian thinking, that I wanted to share our mutual insights widely. I believed that the public deserves to know about the real Jesus—how he perceived himself, and his purpose on Earth. But it wasn't going to happen through Sebastian's own work, which is written on a level suited to those with an advanced theological education. He felt that his complex, deep, and scholarly writing was not for a wide readership, nor was it his calling or forte to write for such a readership. He is one of those seminal thinkers whom others come along later to expand upon.

My first thought was that he and I should coauthor a book. We talked of this, but when I presented my first draft for him to build upon, he realized how different our styles were. It was at this point that Sebastian graciously suggested that I present the material as my own. Since then, this book has evolved to the point where there is truly a blending of my insights with the amazing revelations that he has shared with me.

On the occasion of my first visit with Sebastian, he began reading to me from the Introduction of a book called *The Power of Now*, by Eckhart Tolle. I had not come across this book, but I immediately realized that Eckhart was presenting, from a quite different perspective, the essential insights that Sebastian and I had both come to see through our study of Jesus.

In due course, I submitted my manuscript to Constance Kellough, Publisher of *The Power of Now*.

While on the one hand I cannot express too strongly how this book would never have come into being without Sebastian Moore, neither would it have come into existence without Constance Kellough. Not only did she recognize the value of the work, she also contributed enormously from her own insights, in turn spurring further insights for me.

Constance brought a practicality to the book. In particular, she helped me explain how a person actually enters into the experience of the Christ nature. Her gifts as an editor also assisted me in producing a text that is easily readable by anyone.

And so now, from the publisher of *The Power of Now* comes the same essential insight concerning the divine nature of our humanity, only this time grounded in the life of Jesus.

1

WHY JESUS
IS IMPORTANT TODAY

—

It's Christmas. As Sherry makes her way to the store, her attention is drawn to the elaborate decorations adorning people's houses. It makes her think back to all the years she too focused on the glitter and tinsel of the season.

How often had she bought gifts she couldn't afford, only to see them sit on shelves unused? She thinks of the times she spent half her paycheck trying to make people happier at work. Yet, these relationships never proved anything but empty.

Sherry has cancer, and it's altered how she looks at life. "Three people each sent me $50 so that I could go see the ocean before I die," she says. "I thanked them, but decided to give the money to an organization that provides food for those in need, because seeing the ocean just doesn't seem as important as feeding someone who is hungry. When I get to heaven, I will see the ocean."

To Sherry, heaven is a place where there will be no more pain, she'll never have to battle weight, and she'll always be healthy. Above all, she expects to feel love and contentment.

Sitting in front of the television, Sherry's chemo-drenched brain turns to the suffering in the world around her. She knows about pain. She wishes Jesus would come soon to end all pain.

"I know that what matters is getting as close to the Lord as I can," she says. "Not because of being ill, but because our common goal should be to work toward eternity."

Sherry's heart floods with grief. Though she tries not to, it gets the better of her, and she begins to weep. When she's filled up her wastebasket with tissues, she asks, "Lord, why can't you just come back and take us home?"

YOU CAN EXPERIENCE HEAVEN TODAY

Home. It's a place you feel safe and warm, where you take your shoes off and relax, where you unwind and can be at peace.

People speak of going to heaven as "going home." To finally rest from all the struggles of life is how lots of us think of heaven.

Yet, Jesus seemed to imply that there is a "rest" we can enjoy *here and now.* "Come to Me, all you who labor and are heavy laden," he invited, "and I will give you rest." He added that if we are united with him, life *itself* can be restful. It becomes easy, and its burdens light, he said.

I find few who experience life as restful, easy, light. Sherry's heartfelt cry, "Lord, can't you just come back and take us home?" mirrors a longing in the hearts of many.

In the New Testament, a letter to the Hebrews lists men and women of faith who lived prior to the coming of Jesus—people such as Noah, Abraham and Sarah, Isaac, and Jacob. None of these people were at home in the world, says the writer. Rather, they felt as if they were "strangers and pilgrims on the earth."

Like Sherry, such people were seeking "a homeland" that would be "a heavenly country," but they could never find it. Yet, Jesus assures us that this heavenly homeland is available to you and me today. Indeed, the letter to the Ephesians insists that you and I are, right now, seated "in the heavenly places."

Heaven is here, at this very moment. So much so that we have already been blessed "with *every* spiritual blessing in the heavenly places."

Did you catch that? Every blessing the heavenly dimension can give you is already yours. There is nothing to add—you already have it all!

So why don't you *feel* like you are in heaven?

When I first moved to the United States from England, I had difficulty adjusting to driving on the right side of the road. Many a time I found myself turning into the wrong lane at a junction or when coming out of a driveway. Only when I saw oncoming traffic did I realize my mistake.

Imagine if I told myself, "Since I keep turning onto the wrong side of the road, I must still be in England."

Our *perception* of ourselves can be very different from the truth about ourselves. When we see how flawed we are, it's easy to draw erroneous conclusions about ourselves. This is where faith comes in. Changing how we look at our lives is what faith is all about. It's trusting something is so, even when we sometimes do things that might look the opposite.

The fact is, I *had* moved from England to the United States, and my lapses into the way I had driven for years didn't place me back in Britain. As my identification with America grew and it began to feel natural to drive on the other side of the road, I stopped turning into the wrong lane altogether. I had become one with my new country.

In her suffering, Sherry wants to draw closer to the Lord. Like so many of us, she doesn't realize that it's only a question of opening our eyes to see what's already true. God is here with us at this moment, in all of the richness of the heavenly experience.

This was the message of Jesus. It's just as relevant today as when the people of Galilee first heard it 2,000 years ago, for it speaks to the longing of the human heart to find our home in God.

THE PROMISED LAND IS WITHIN YOU

We call him Jesus, but he was never called this in his lifetime. Joseph and Mary were told to name him "savior," meaning "deliverer." In Hebrew, this is Yeshua. Jesus is the Greek equivalent of Yeshua. Had they spoken English, Jesus' family and disciples would have called him Joshua.

The name Joshua evoked images of the powerful successor to Moses in the Hebrew story of the exodus and Israel's conquest of the promised land. It was Joshua, not Moses, who led the people into the promised land after their years of hard labor in Egypt. But even though Joshua succeeded where Moses failed, this promised land didn't turn out to be the restful home the people longed for. Daily life in Palestine continued to be full of turmoil.

In Israel everyone observed a weekly day of rest called the Sabbath. The New Testament letter to the Hebrews asserts that both the land of promise and this weekly Sabbath picture the peaceful state God intends people to enjoy—though neither the Sabbath nor the land of promise are able to deliver this peace.

Jesus, the "new" Joshua, recognized that God's peace isn't found in a particular place or day. Rather, he found it deep within *himself*. This enabled him to enjoy a continual peace. He was able to relax and let go of all worry. Instead of being filled with fear, his life was full of promise.

Through their contact with their new Joshua, Jesus' disciples came to realize that the promised land isn't of this world. It isn't a material state, the result of any kind of external circumstance. Rather, it's a state of mind in which we are awakened to the dimension of God within ourselves.

Jesus embodied the restful state his disciples had longed for all their lives. As they came to understand themselves in the way their "new" Joshua understood himself, their lives too took on the calm of the Sabbath.

Finding themselves increasingly "at home" in themselves, they started to become their own promised land.

IT'S ALL ABOUT AWARENESS

How does a person enter into this internal promised land, this Sabbath that is of the spirit?

Said the New Testament author Paul of Tarsus, God gives to all life, breath, and all things. The promised land is entered, and its Sabbath enjoyed, when we become *aware of God* in every breath we take, everything around us, and all that makes up our daily existence. How can we not be at peace if God is the source of every aspect of our lives?

Paul went further. He insisted that "*in*" God we live, and move, and have our being. How can there be anything at all to fret about when not just parts of your life, but every aspect of your life is infused with the divine presence?

Nothing you do happens outside of God. How could it, when every breath you take, every movement you make, takes place "in" God?

When this realization takes hold of you, not just on an intellectual level but deep in your being, it frees you from all anxiety about yourself and your life. It erases all guilt—all sense of somehow being unacceptable. It's the end of having to hide or be embarrassed about any part of your life. You can relax and simply *be*, knowing that you are part of the infinite presence we call God.

It also ends the feeling of emptiness that causes life to seem unfulfilling. "I have come that they may have life," said Jesus, "and that they may have it more abundantly." He wasn't speaking of a fulfillment beyond the grave. Rather, he showed us that it's possible to live a heavenly life now. Isn't this what we are all seeking?

Sherry wants to prepare herself for eternity. Yet Jesus said that whoever believes in him will "never die." We are *already* in eternity. To experience eternal life is to recognize God's presence in each moment of your life.

When you truly accept the presence of God in *you*, you are in the promised land.

2

JESUS SHOWS YOU
WHO YOU ARE

—

What are humans, that God pays attention to them? asks an ancient author.

What's so wonderful about you? Why would God be interested in you?

In answer to his question, this author points us to Jesus. If you look to Jesus, he says, you will discover who *you* really are.

The person who wrote this letter to the Hebrews describes Jesus as the "captain" of a journey each of us is taking toward wholeness. Or, as other translations put it, he has "pioneered" the path of our potential.

If we look closely at Jesus, what do we see?

Jesus is introduced to us in four gospels. Rather than being detailed historical records of his life, these gospels are portraits in words. A portrait is quite different from a snapshot of a historical moment. Whereas a snapshot offers a glimpse of a particular event frozen in time, a portrait seeks to capture something of the essence of the person.[1]

The portraits of Jesus in the gospels are presented by people whose lives, either directly or indirectly, had been changed by him. In their portraits of him, we can see just how earthshaking this change was. They wanted their readers to understand what it was about Jesus that affected them so deeply.

It's clear that Jesus had a magnetic effect on his disciples. To be around him was magical. But what they experienced in his presence wasn't just his charisma as a personality. The real draw was that he awakened in them an aspect of *themselves* of which they had been unaware.

The portraits of Jesus painted by the disciples invite us to see him in a way that makes possible a new understanding of ourselves.

EXPERIENCING GOD IN YOURSELF

Though their spiritual tradition said they were sons and daughters of God, in the very image of God, this meant little to most Judeans. But Jesus introduced people to their divine likeness as a *life-changing experience*.

Religion has traditionally portrayed God as separate from us. God made everything, and we are inferior creatures who must grovel before this awesome Being.

Jesus had no such picture of God.

The nature of God was something the religious leaders of Jesus' day wanted to argue about with him, but he refused. Instead of debating about God, what Jesus offered people was simply himself. He was a living example of a person who knew himself to be grounded in God. If you have seen me, he said, you have seen God.

Because the religious leaders thought of God as quite separate from themselves, they accused Jesus of blasphemy. How could a mere man call himself God?

Jesus could claim to reveal the nature of God because he knew God intimately. In fact, God was more real to him than anything else. He knew God intuitively, and his intuitive knowledge of God gave him insight into everything else in his life.

Jesus knew that God is beyond conceptualizing. Centuries earlier, the Hebrew prophets had also realized this about God. This is why the religious tradition Jesus was born into shunned representations of God, such as statues and pictures. God isn't something that can be imagined, and to liken God to anything misses God entirely.

But somehow the notion that God is an imaginable person prevailed. People yearned to make the incomprehensible comprehensible. God became the Big Person who made the world, the Great Architect.

Jesus knew that when we talk about God as a separate being, we fail to talk about God at all. Such an idea of God is pure imagination. If God is infinite, God couldn't possibly be a being. Any such being, however big we might imagine this being, would still be finite.

To speak of God as a being is referring to that which gives existence to *everything* as though it too were *something*.[2]

When Jesus spoke of God, he meant something very different from what most people mean. For him, God was nothing that we can point to. God doesn't have the kind of concrete reality that normally grabs our minds, and therefore doesn't strike us in the way other things do.

The religious tradition Jesus inherited said that God created the world out of emptiness. God is a reservoir of infinite possibilities, out of which *all* things emerge and in which everything happens.

It's this ability to be both *beyond* everything and *in* everything simultaneously that makes God unidentifiable.

HOW JESUS KNEW HE WAS ONE WITH GOD

We want to be able to imagine God so that God seems real. But by trying to make God seem real and somehow closer to us, we deny ourselves the one access to God that is available.[3]

Though God cannot be described and is beyond our comprehension, Jesus sensed that God is familiar to us. While God isn't a being like other beings, and can't be imagined, Jesus realized that God is *personal*. In fact, he was certain that *God is the most personal reality there is.*

Jesus called God *abba*, the Hebrew word for "daddy." He spoke of God in this way because God is the essence of all persons. To be a person is to be an expression of God.

We cannot *point* to God as a separate entity, but we can *know* God. What does it mean to "know" God?

Our minds experience a constant state of background awareness, or consciousness. This background awareness precedes our awareness of specific things. We are never without this background awareness.

It's even present in our sleep, noticing our dreams. All of our awareness of specific things is grounded in it.

Have you ever had an "Aha!" feeling? You read something or someone says something to you, and suddenly you know that you knew it
all along. It was in the background of your awareness, but you weren't
directly aware of it.

Knowing something before you can bring it to mind is a common
experience. For instance, you know there's a word for what you want
to say, but you can't quite put your finger on it. The person you are
talking to coaxes you, "Come on, you can think of it!"

"I've nearly got it," you say. You can feel that it's on the tip of your
tongue. And yet, it doesn't come. But a short time later, when you are
no longer trying to think of the word, it pops into your mind.

Sensing that you know something before you can actually think of
it is a form of direct knowing. This direct knowing, which many refer
to as their intuition, allows us to know something for certain without
the support of either logic or sensory experience.

It's in this sense that we can know God. The divine is known only
in an indescribable, intuitive way, behind our surface thoughts. It's a
kind of knowing that has no emotion to it. You are very calm, and you
just know that you know.

Jesus took a step that was contrary to every belief of his culture. He
acknowledged that the essence of our humanity, behind our surface
thoughts and emotions, is in fact God. This was the breakthrough that
enabled him to recognize that he was God incarnate.

As Jesus got in touch with his Christ essence, the "knowing" that
had been in the background came into the foreground. He stepped
into *direct* knowing.

Most of us hold back from taking this leap. In fact, we prevent ourselves from accessing such direct knowing. We continually tell ourselves, "I don't know!" Then we either react to a situation emotionally,
or we try to think our way through it and hope we come up with the
right answer.

In fact, we *do* know—we know everything we need to know at any
given moment. It's in the background of our awareness. And, just like

trying to think of a word, it will spring into consciousness if, instead of trying to think our way to a solution, we become relaxed and at peace with ourselves. As Jesus said, his way comes *easily*. There is no agonizing, no struggle, no indecisiveness. There is simply a sureness born of a deep calm.

We all have the ability to experience direct knowing any time we need to know what to do. This is what Jesus was showing us when he said, "Do not worry about how or what you should speak. For it will be given to you in that hour what you should speak; for it is not you who speak, but the Spirit of your Father who speaks in you." Your essence, which is God, knows *just* what is needed *at the right moment*.

Why do we think that we don't know? Well, it's like learning to ride a bicycle. When you first get on a bicycle, staying upright without your feet on the ground feels all but impossible. You tell yourself, "I'll never get the hang of this." But if you transcend your thoughts and the anxiety they generate, with a little practice you discover that balancing on two wheels is really quite easy.

You had the ability to ride all along, but you simply hadn't accessed this ability. It's all a matter of confidence—faith in yourself. Once the skill of balancing on two wheels has been accessed, you never again doubt your ability to ride a bicycle, no matter how long it is since the last time you were on one.

While Jesus taught that God can't be identified as a separate reality, he insisted that God can be experienced. He realized that in truly knowing *himself*, he knew God. His self-awareness was the wellspring of his knowledge of God.

JESUS LIVED IN THE PROMISED REST

To encounter a person who knew himself to be one with God had an overwhelming effect on those who were close to Jesus.

For a start, they had never been around anyone who was so calm. Jesus was so collected that his followers later described him as possessing a peace "which surpasses all understanding." He lived the life of the promised land every day. His mode of being was that of a continual Sabbath.

Many of us live stressful lives and yearn for a sense of peace. There are times when we have to get away from it all—into the peace of the countryside, the silence of the mountains, or the serenity of the seashore. But no sooner do we return to the daily grind than we again feel stressed. A lasting sense of peace is hard to come by.

When Jesus spent time alone, it wasn't because he had to have space or he would "lose it." Even under the intense stress of arrest, trial, and crucifixion, he could remain composed and fully in control of himself. His sense of peace never left him. His times alone were opportunities for reflection, as a preparation for his mission. In the Garden of Gethsemane, Jesus' agony, in which he sweat drops of blood, did not reflect his state of being, which continued to be non-reactive, but his need to gain absolute clarity concerning this final act of his mission.

If Jesus' calmness amazed the disciples, so did his immense joy.

All of us have moments when we are happy. But feeling "happy" when things are going well is quite different from the joy that flowed through Jesus.

Joy is a state of being. It's a sensation of ecstasy, a feeling of rapture. You can't help jumping, shouting, skipping, dancing, because you can't contain this kind of joy. Jesus exuded this joy in such an unbridled manner that it was truly an experience of seeing God just to be around him. This sheer joy of being alive isn't how we feel most of the time. If we experience such a "high," it's usually through sex, drugs, adventure, or perhaps closing a big business deal.

With Jesus, joy was the undercurrent of his life, present even in those periods when everything seemed to be going wrong. On the eve of his death he told his followers, "These things I have spoken to you so that My *joy* may remain in you, and that your joy may be *full*." Jesus wanted his disciples to experience the rapture, the ecstasy that never left him regardless of circumstances.

The disciples were also attracted by Jesus' incredible certainty. He was the first person they had met who had no reservations about himself. It was as if all normal human defenses were absent in this man.

Without mask or pretense and utterly transparent, his followers saw a person who, unlike what they experienced in themselves and other people, had no self-doubt whatever. He didn't bad-mouth himself, didn't put himself down, didn't feel inferior to anyone.

Once he knew who he was, Jesus was able to chart his own course in life with boldness. His confidence came from within, without requiring the validation of anyone else. He didn't need his mother, his brothers, or his disciples to confirm his decisions. He didn't need anyone else's opinions.

Jesus' wonderful sense of himself meant he could be himself with complete freedom. He put on no airs. He was entirely natural. Secure within himself, he had no need to impress anyone. Delighting in himself, he was supremely attractive as a personality and must have been utterly enchanting to be around.

It was clear to the disciples that Jesus felt loved and altogether lovable. Yet he wasn't "in love with himself" in the high-and-mighty way that people who are self-absorbed are in love with themselves. On the contrary, he shocked his followers by washing their dusty feet, which was the work of a common servant. He was simply loving them in the way he felt loved.

Jesus' sense of joy, confidence, calmness, and delight in himself was contagious. The effect was to invite people to experience this for themselves. Slowly, the disciples began to awaken to a previously unrecognized peace at their center. They discovered a joy that they had once felt as children. As their awareness of their beauty, desirability, and attractiveness increased, their feelings of inferiority decreased.

Like Jesus, you are God's son or daughter. This means God's own nature is present in you, just as it was in Jesus. Jesus seeks to introduce you to this reality. In doing so, he introduces you to God as an all-embracing reality that you discover as your *own* reality, rather than as an external reality to which you are supposed to pay homage.

3

WHAT IS THE SECOND COMING?

—

So troubled was the world of Jesus' time, and so deep in despair were the populace, that it was commonly believed that nothing short of divine intervention could change things. People spoke of this hoped-for intervention as the kingdom of God. They imagined the kingdom coming in one fell swoop, as many do today.

While the masses in Jesus' day were looking for God to send a messiah to rescue them, Jesus introduced his followers to the kingdom as the expression of an invisible presence that lies at the heart of reality. Instead of viewing the depressing condition of the world as something only a divine intervention could change, he insisted that God's reign could begin in people's lives any time they were ready to awaken to this Presence. It's "at hand," he explained, there to be grasped. Don't look for God to appear in the desert or on a mountaintop, because the kingdom isn't about location. Instead, "The kingdom of God is *within you.*"

This wasn't a message most people of Jesus' time wanted to hear. They wanted a champion who would deliver them. Though Jesus stated clearly that the kingdom was an inward reality, not an earthly empire, for a long time even his disciples failed to grasp what he was really saying. They couldn't free themselves from the centuries-old expectation that the messiah would conquer Israel's enemies and usher in an era of peace and well-being. They sought a literal promised land and failed to accept that Jesus' way of ushering in the kingdom of God wasn't through violent political revolution but via a revolution of the heart.

HEAVEN COMES TO EARTH

Because the Kingdom is both an individual and collective reality, the full extent of God's kingdom can't be experienced until all participate in it. God's magnificence will be fully seen only when God's presence is experienced in everyone.[4]

When is the kingdom to be revealed?

As God's presence is more fully experienced in each of us, the kingdom becomes a reality.

Jesus likened the coming of the kingdom to the action of yeast in bread. The yeast grows until the whole loaf has risen. In the same way, as increasing numbers of us experience the reign of Christ in our lives, the kingdom becomes more and more present until it gradually fills the whole earth.

On the eve of his crucifixion, Jesus told his disciples that he was going away to prepare a place for them. He was referring to the "heavenly places" in which, according to the letter to Ephesus, we are presently seated with him.

If he went, Jesus said, he would "come again," so that where he is, we may be also. Most translations distort the Greek, so that this statement is often read at funerals as if it refers to a coming beyond the grave. But the Greek employs a continuous tense that has the sense of a *continual appearing*. The second "coming" is an ongoing process of revelation of God's presence in humanity.[5]

When you catch onto this, it's like being born again, born a second time, born "from above" as Jesus put it.[6] You start to function from awareness of God's presence in you, instead of from your troubled thoughts and torn emotions. You become a reflection of God in the world, mirroring the majesty of the Creator.

For you this *is* the second coming. The divine presence exemplified in Jesus has come alive in you. It's as if Jesus were walking the earth all over again.

JESUS INVITES US TO LOOK WITHIN

Jesus told Nicodemus, a leader in Israel, that you can't even "see" this realm of which he was speaking until your inner eyes are opened. But once you see your oneness with God, you are, in the words of the letter to the Colossians, delivered "from the power of darkness" and conveyed "into the kingdom of the Son of His love." Nothing in life is ever the same again. The dull, dreary drudgery of everyday existence is transformed into a glorious experience because you see everything, including the most simple things, in a new light.

It's important to recognize that the term "kingdom" is an outdated metaphor in our more democratic world. Jesus didn't literally see God as a king who decrees how we should live our lives.

On the contrary, in Jesus' view a profound sense of God's involvement in our lives leads not to subservience but to *freedom*. "If the Son makes you free," he said, "you shall be free indeed." Instead of thinking of God as a ruler who tells us what to do, he saw God's presence in us as freeing us to be like himself. As he said on the eve of his crucifixion, we aren't his servants, inferior to him, we are his friends.

The kingdom of God is available to you to the degree you know yourself to be an expression of the divine presence that pervades everything. The kingdom arrives as you take charge of your life, not in an egoistic way, but empowered by the divine presence. As the book of Revelation says repeatedly, you are an "overcomer." You overcome all obstacles that block the full expression of God's presence in you.

The presence at the heart of your being, hidden beneath layers of self-doubt, begins to "rule" your life, and you experience God's kingdom. You become fully engaged in each and every moment of your life. In the words of the letter to the Romans, you "reign in life."

To be a part of the kingdom is the end of your world as you've known it. For you, an entirely new world comes into being. The kingdom of heaven has come to earth in *you*, in answer to the prayer, "Your kingdom come, Your will be done on earth as it is in heaven." You embody the presence of God in the world.

4

GOD HAS ONLY ONE SON— AND YOU ARE PART OF HIM

—

A minister of a large denominational church issued a hypothetical challenge to the minister of a small independent fellowship. "If I were to let you address my congregation," he challenged, "what would you say, in twenty seconds or less, that would be a revelation to them?"

The minister thought for a moment. What could he impart to these people that they didn't already believe?

"I'd share an amazing truth that's been overlooked by most of the religious world for 2,000 years," said the minister. "There are only two humans on earth. They are *Adam* and *Christ*. Just as Adam is a *body* of people, encompassing the whole human race, *so also the Christ is a body of people*. In fact, the Christ is a potential in *all* humans, for Paul said that as in Adam all die, even so in Christ all shall be made alive."

Did you realize that Adam and Christ are not simply individuals, but terms used to describe the history and destiny of the human race? They include *your* history and destiny.

So it is that the New Testament speaks of the *body* of Christ. This collective reality is made up of all who have become conscious of their oneness with God. When this awareness takes over our lives, we become a more evolved human, as was Jesus. He represents the next leap in our development as a species.

As awareness of our oneness with God increases, the impact isn't just personal. It changes how we relate to each other. Recognition of our oneness with God leads to oneness among us. All barriers between the world's peoples are broken down. The future of the human species involves the gathering together of all races and creeds to form, as the letter to the Ephesians puts it, *one new human being*. This collective "one new human being"[7] is the Christ.

THE CHRIST IS A NEW HUMANITY

The inclusive nature of the Christ can be seen in a title Jesus often applied to himself: "The Son of Man." This figure isn't just an individual but is comprised of a body of people.[8]

The Christ is referred to as the *Son* of Man because this body of people emerges out of our humanity and transcends our humanness as we have so far known it.

Paul explained that the first Adam became "a living being." As a part of the Adamic race, we experience life on a certain level. On the surface, we look like an advanced form of animal life. At this level, many find it a struggle just to make it from day to day. The lives of a great many humans are difficult to bear.

But Paul went on to speak of a "last Adam" who became "a life-giving spirit." The term "last Adam" has a dual meaning. It's an individual, and it's corporate. Individually, the last Adam is Jesus of Nazareth, who embodies the Christ nature. Collectively, *the last Adam is all in whom the Christ nature is presently being birthed.*

Let me hasten to add that the term "last," as Paul uses it, has a different meaning from its common usage. Jesus, the head of the body of people known as the Christ, is the embodiment of God-consciousness. As such he epitomizes what the Adamic race was always meant to be and is destined to become. He is definitive of—the measure of—what it is to be truly human in a way that reflects the divine, as all humans are meant to do. In him we see what humanity, infused with God-consciousness, looks like. Hence he points to the "final" form of our humanity. It's in this sense that Paul calls him the last Adam.

Adam was the representative of humanity as we have come to know ourselves. Jesus is the representative of the new humanity that God is raising up out of our existing state of being. The term "Christ" points to that life in us that is so much more than the life we presently know.

We don't see our potential, and throughout most of history have been taught to deny its very existence. Traditionally, societies have stressed that we "know our place." Most of us learn to see ourselves as just average, certainly nothing special. This is why we need Jesus. He functions as a mirror of our potential. In him we see a reflection of who we really are.

Ponder for a moment the expression life-giving spirit. This evolved species of humans live a life powered by spirit—by a deep awareness of God in everyone and everything. When this reality guides your every day, you don't long to escape your life. You are *full* of life. As Jesus experienced and wants us to experience, life flows in abundance. You are in the promised land.

BEGOTTEN, NOT CREATED

The Gospel of John speaks of God's only begotten Son. The term "begotten" means generated from within God's own being, rather than created as a separate entity in the way that we might make something with our hands.

The word "only" is used both in a definitive sense and in an *inclusive* sense.

Used definitively, "only" means, "This is what God is like, and not something else." The only begotten son is the spitting image of God, which will ultimately be expressed in all humans.

The second meaning of "only" parallels the title Son of Man, in that it's one reality composed of many members. The "only begotten Son of God" isn't separate from us, it's inclusive of us. Collectively we make up God's only begotten son.[9]

The term begotten is important because, as was the case with Jesus, it means we aren't simply something God made. Rather, we emerge from God and reflect who God is. As the letter to the Hebrews says, the Son, epitomized in Jesus and filled out in all of us, is the brightness of

God's glory and the express *image of His person*. Our essence is God's essence. Though we have manifested it only sporadically, it has been in us from the beginning.

In modern language we might speak of this essence of humanity as the *blueprint* for what our species is in process of becoming. It's in this sense that the letter to the Colossians says of Jesus, in whom this essence is fully fleshed out, that he is the *firstborn* over *all* creation. We are being invited to undergo a metamorphosis through which we are to become just like Jesus.

In other words, God's essence is what has guided the emergence of the entire universe, especially humans, culminating in the coming of Jesus and the new kind of human he embodies.[10] This new kind of human is destined to become the universal experience of humanity.

GOD BECOMES VISIBLE

God is invisible. No one has seen God at any time, the Gospel of John tells us.

Yet Jesus asserted, "He who has seen Me has seen the Father." How could Jesus claim that if people had seen him, they had seen God? How can you see something invisible?

The New Testament often speaks of God as light. Consider the nature of light. You can't see light, though it allows you to see everything else. But if light passes through a prism, it bursts into a rainbow of colors and becomes visible.

Though God is invisible, God can be "seen" through the prism of all of life.

Jesus understood himself to be a visible expression of the invisible. "I am the light of the world," he said. This is why he could insist that in seeing him, people were seeing God.

In the Sermon on the Mount Jesus said of you and me, "You are the light of the world." Each of us is an expression of the infinite, a colorful ray that contains all of God and at the same time reveals a unique aspect of our Creator.

Together with Jesus we make up the image and likeness of God. Or as the letter to Ephesus puts it, as a collective body we express "the fullness of Him who fills all in all." This is a stunning statement. Dwell on it for a moment. We are the *fullness* of God made manifest.

Talk about a sense of identity! In that we derive our nature from God, we are "chips off the old block." We emerged from God and we have no being other than God.

YOU ARE AN EXPRESSION OF GOD

God's essence is expressed in every part of the universe and has been since time began. But we don't really get a true picture of this emerging essence until humans inhabit the earth. In Jesus it reaches its apex. He was a forerunner of who we are all becoming. As Paul wrote to the Romans, Jesus is the "firstborn among *many*" brothers and sisters.

This is why Paul speaks of each of us becoming "conformed to the image" of God's son. This is a process of unveiling our true being, which is shown to us in Jesus. Although in our essence we are "complete in Christ," lacking nothing because we have been blessed with every spiritual blessing in the heavenly dimension, our essence still awaits full manifestation. Consequently, we sometimes feel less than complete. Who we really are has to be drawn out until it rules our everyday lives.

In life's difficult times, it helps to know that everything we go through is intended to bring out the Christ nature in us. As Paul put it, the whole creation groans and labors with *birth pangs*. It's easier to cope with the difficulties you experience when you realize they are all part of birthing your Christ nature.

In fact, Paul was convinced that none of the pain of the world is purposeless. How comforting it is to know that *everything* that happens is happening in God. It's all happening with the objective of "the *revealing* of the sons of God." We are assured that we shall finally be, in everyday life, the glorious individuals we *already* are in our essential being.

TOGETHER WE ARE THE CHRIST

When the people of Corinth were caught up in patterns of old behavior that didn't reflect who they really were, Paul had to remind them that whoever is joined to the Lord is "*one* spirit" with him. The Corinthians had lost sight of their oneness with the Christ. This is a common experience, and the reason many of us don't experience the glorious life God intends for us. Although we can never be separated from our essence as the Christ, it takes experience to realize this and begin living in accord with it.

Paul didn't immediately find that he could live from his essence either. As we shall see in Chapter 7, he went through quite a struggle before his Christ nature became evident in his daily life. But in due course, his Christ nature was so complete that he could assert, "For to me, to live *is Christ*." This is an amazing statement. So identified with the Christ nature was Paul that for him to go about his daily life was just like Jesus being here all over again!

"For to me, to live *is Christ*" means that Christ had returned, in the form of Paul.

Paul had undergone a radical reevaluation of his identity, to the extent that the person he had always *thought* he was "no longer" lived. Instead, "*Christ* lives in me."

It's this transformation that the letter to the Colossians points to when it speaks of "Christ in *you*, the hope of *glory*." It's tempting to think of "glory" as something in the future. But this is a hope that we can realistically expect to see fulfilled here and now. We are meant to experience the love, joy, and peace of the promised land each and every day, not sometime way off in the future.

Jesus stressed the immediacy of God's glory when he said on the night of his arrest, "And the *glory* which You gave Me *I have given them*." God's glory isn't something that lies in the future. It has already been given to us, and it is in process of being revealed.

The Christ nature comes into view only as we dare to *believe* in it. We shall see in the course of this book how such belief is born in us.

Jesus prayed that each of us might experience the *identical* oneness with God that he personally enjoyed. "*As you*, Father, are in me, and I in you; that *they* may be one in Us," is how he put it. We are to see ourselves as one with Jesus, and thus one with God, *in the same way that Jesus saw himself* as one with God. For Paul this became an everyday reality.

Although few seem to experience the Christ nature as Paul did, Jesus meant it to become our everyday reality also. In the same prayer, he said, "I in them, and You in Me, that they may be *perfect* in one." We are to manifest the Christ nature not sporadically, but continuously.

And it's all a matter of *correct perception.*

When you cease seeing the essence of Jesus as separate from your own essence, and recognize that like him you participate in the divine essence, the same powerful consciousness that pervaded the life of Jesus becomes your everyday mindset. Your life flows peacefully, effortlessly, restfully.

You live a life that is a daily Sabbath.

5

YOUR ESSENTIAL
GOODNESS

—

To most Christians the idea that God dwells within them, and therefore they are essentially good, is unthinkable. On the contrary, many insist, all are stained with original sin. Were it not for God's mercy, we would be damned.

REINFORCING FEELINGS OF INFERIORITY

Though their spiritual tradition said that they were created in the image of God, the people of Judea thought of themselves as far below God. They felt unworthy even to approach God.

The idea that people are unworthy was reinforced by two institutions of Judean society that were constant reminders to people of their lowly state. These were the temple and the Sabbath.

The temple was considered God's house and therefore holy ground. It consisted of a series of courtyards and rooms, one inside the other. God was believed to live in the innermost room, which was so holy that none but the high priest could enter, and then only once a year. On this one day of the year, the high priest was required to fast from sunset, when the Jews began their day, until the following sunset, when that day ended. He abstained not only from food but also from water. Only after undergoing ritual cleansings, donning special clothing, and offering sacrifices could he enter.

In the second most holy room was a sacred altar on which fresh consecrated bread was placed each day. No ordinary person could eat this bread. To serve at this altar you had to be a priest from a specially chosen family, cleansed by ritual washings, and made worthy by the offering of sacrifices.

As the temple represented holy ground, which ordinary humans were believed to be unfit to step on, so the weekly Sabbath represented holy time. From Friday sunset through Saturday sunset all unnecessary human activities were suspended. It wasn't permissible to light a fire for cooking. It was even forbidden to carry anything at all.

JESUS REJECTED THE IDEA OF INFERIORITY

Jesus scandalized his society by showing that the idea that God considers humans inferior is nonsense. He repudiated the common belief that people are on a lesser plane than God.

To make his point, one Sabbath Jesus took a walk through a grain field with his disciples. As they strolled through the field, the disciples became hungry and plucked ears of grain. Jesus approved of what they were doing. When the religious authorities saw this, they charged Jesus with encouraging his followers to desecrate the Sabbath.

Jesus responded with two precedents from Israel's sacred scriptures. In the first, King David, the founder of the nation of Israel, violated sacred space. When he and his companions were hungry, they entered God's house and ate the sacred bread that only the priests were permitted to eat. In the second, priests at work in the temple on the Sabbath violated sacred time. The law itself prescribed that priests perform the laborious tasks required to offer sacrifices on the Sabbath.

Jesus' point was that humans are more important than either sacred space or sacred time. He defended the right of his followers to ignore any law that treated humans as inferior to God.

As if to make his point still more bluntly, Jesus then entered the synagogue on the Sabbath and healed a man with a withered hand, which provoked an outcry from the religious authorities. It galled them that Jesus saw himself, his disciples, and those he helped as far more important than holy places and holy days.

The authorities profited from keeping the masses trapped in low self-esteem. They knew that people who believe they aren't worth much don't demand much. Threatened by Jesus' powerful sense of self and the way he was empowering others, the religious leaders set in motion a conspiracy to eliminate him.

Jesus saw that telling people they are fundamentally flawed causes untold harm. Knowing himself to be good, he was out of step with his society, which believed that people are evil. He challenged this prevailing view of our humanity by pointing to the dignity of our humanity, showing that we are more worthy than even the holiest of items in the temple or the holy time of the Sabbath.[11]

In this same context, Jesus said of the religious leaders who criticized him for valuing humans above the nation's sacred institutions, that, "being evil," they could not be expected to say good things about anybody. Because they saw themselves as evil, the actions of these leaders turned out to be evil much of the time.

Jesus' words, "being evil," do not describe the essential state of humanity, only the condition of the religious leaders who had become corrupt because of their distorted view of their humanity. On the contrary, Jesus went on to say that while evil came out of the hearts—the thoughts—of these leaders, similarly a good person out of the good treasure of his or her heart brings forth good things.

Jesus reinforced this understanding of our humanity on another occasion, when he asked, "If you then, being evil, know how to give good gifts to your children, how much more will your Father who is in heaven give good things to those who ask Him?" Again, "being evil" refers to the leaders in their corrupted state, which resulted from how they saw themselves. Yet, even in this state, they still often did good things! No human is essentially evil, and even the Hitlers of the world do a few good things as evidence of their long forgotten true self.

On one occasion, a person spoke of Jesus as "good." Jesus used the opportunity to make the point that God alone is good. For Jesus to be good, he must be divine! But if Jesus, whom this inquirer considered to be a man, was divine, then the point the inquirer took home with him is that Jesus believed our humanity to be Godlike!

Jesus defended his flagrant disregard for those elements of religion that lessen human dignity by claiming that he and God were "one." He was saying that humanity and divinity are intrinsically the same. Though the spiritual tradition of the Judean people said that humans were God's offspring, Jesus seems to have been alone in realizing that this means a human is equal to God.

Upon hearing him claim to be "one" with God, the authorities picked up stones, intent on carrying out a public execution. Jesus pointed to the good works he had done, then challenged, "For which of those works do you stone Me?"

The authorities explained that it wasn't for anything he'd done that they were going to stone him, "but for blasphemy, and because You, being a Man, make Yourself God."

To the charge of blasphemy, Jesus responded by citing the sacred scriptures: "Is it not written in your law, 'I said, You are gods'?"

Jesus' argument was impossible to refute. The authorities knew that according to scripture, everyone is "god," in the sense that we are all daughters or sons of God and hence divine. If all are divine, how could Jesus be guilty of blasphemy for claiming to be God's son?

I want to emphasize that Jesus' argument ran in exactly the opposite direction from how we usually think of his divinity. He didn't claim to be uniquely divine, which is the common view. On the contrary, *he could claim to be divine because scripture said all humans are divine!*

"SIN" DOESN'T CHANGE YOUR ESSENCE

Is it difficult to believe that humans share in the divine nature? Perhaps you are willing to allow this in the case of Jesus, but not for yourself. Surely humans have far too many flaws to be like him?

The followers of Jesus who recorded his message for us realized that in our essential person we mirror God, but in daily life we fall short of our potential to reflect the magnificence of the divine. In each of us, to varying degrees, the mirror has become fogged. Paul, in a letter to the Romans, describes this "fog" as a universal condition. "All have sinned and fall short of the glory of God," he says.

The word sin means "to miss the mark." Think of archers shooting arrows at a target. When we're true to ourselves, like an arrow that hits the bull's eye, we aren't sinful. But, Paul argues, none of us grow up completely true to ourselves. However, he came to realize that we *can* grow into our Christ self to the full extent Jesus did.

In not being true to ourselves, Paul describes us as not matching up to "the *glory* of God." What does it mean to glorify God? Is it not to live to the hilt, fully alive? In Paul's words, "Whether you eat or drink, or whatever you do, do all to the glory of God." When we live life with nothing held back, it becomes a glorious experience.

To live such a glorious life isn't merely a future hope, it's a present possibility. Indeed, it's the way we are meant to live. It's what heaven, the promised land, is all about.

In his final prayer on the eve of his arrest, Jesus said, "The glory which You gave Me *I have given them*, that they may be one *just as We are one.*" Notice the tense—"*have* given." The key to manifesting the glory of God as Jesus did is to awaken to the fact that *we are one with God in the same way he was.*

Why don't we live up to our glorious potential?

A quick answer is that society teaches us to be less than our true selves. While this is so, it doesn't explain how society got to be a place in which humans grow up to be less than they have the ability to be. The explanation requires taking a close look at a belief that's one of the underpinnings of our culture.

Christianity has historically spoken of a "fall," which took place in the Garden of Eden. It is claimed that Adam and Eve rebelled against God. There was a simple choice to be made—obedience or disobedience—and our first parents made the wrong choice.

We are told that Adam and Eve's disobedience changed the basic nature of humans. Ever since, the effects of this "original sin" have been transmitted genetically to all of their descendants, so that humans come into the world tainted with evil. The most innocent-looking child is assumed to have a rebellious heart that's sinful.

RETHINKING THE FALL

When we carefully read the two creation stories at the beginning of Genesis, they don't describe a change in our nature at all. Instead, they tell *how humans came to doubt their worth.*

According to the creation story with which the Bible opens, God created all the creatures of earth to reproduce "after their kind." Birds reproduce birds, fish reproduce fish, and apes reproduce apes, so that each new generation is essentially like the preceding generation.

The statement that creatures reproduce after their kind is an observation about the birds and the bees. Anyone can see that each "kind" reproduces its own kind. This observation is intended to prepare the reader for a spiritual insight concerning the essential nature of humanity. This insight comes in the next statement, where, after creating the various kinds to each reproduce in the image of their kind, God then created humans in the likeness of God's own self. In other words, humans are God's self-reproduction. Humans are created after the "God kind."

What are human beings, that God cares for them, asked the psalmist. The letter to the Hebrews repeats this question, then explains that God has "crowned" us with "glory and honor." If God has crowned us with glory and honor, why would we put ourselves down? Why would we not honor ourselves? Are we better judges of ourselves than our Creator?

Isn't it a little arrogant to imagine we know ourselves better than God knows us? Could it be that we've got it exactly backwards? When Paul told the Romans that "whatever is not from faith is sin," he was saying that we are to live every facet of our lives confidently, not doubtingly. Our self-doubt—our continual questioning of our worthiness—is the very essence of sin.

But aren't we "lower" than God? Only in the sense that Jesus was divine yet spoke of God as "greater" than himself. It's not that we are qualitatively inferior, any more than Jesus was. Rather, we are like any one ray of sunshine, which carries the sun's essence yet isn't the whole glory of the sun.

This is made clear by the author of Hebrews. Quoting the same psalm, he says that God cares about us because, like Jesus, we are sons and daughters of God. So on a par are we with Jesus that he's "not ashamed" to call us brothers and sisters. Brothers and sisters are not different "kinds," but the same.

It may not be evident that we are on a par with Jesus, says Hebrews, because God is still in the process of "bringing many sons unto glory," drawing out our potential. But whether we recognize it or not, Jesus has "captained"—pioneered—the kind of glorious life we are *all* meant to experience.

We come now to the main insight of the first Genesis creation story. The point the author is driving at is that, since humans are an expression of divinity, *we must be intrinsically good!* And so, at the climax of this story, God pronounced all that had come into being "very good."

It's important to notice that at no time does this creation story rescind this verdict. The creation, including humanity, is good. Period. No matter that we fall short of our glorious potential, our behavior doesn't change the *essence* of who we are.

Indeed, God uses our failures to push us to discover our fundamental greatness. Awareness of our inherent divinity doesn't come with our natural birth but is a process of enlightenment—of remembering our God essence.

"SIN" IS FAILING TO BE TRUE TO YOURSELF

To sin is to be untrue to your essence. Humans are true to themselves when they realize that they are created after the "God kind" and live accordingly. Though their tradition taught this, in practice the entire priestly system based on the temple and holy days was designed to show that humans are far beneath God.

Seeing how often people veered from being true to their essential goodness, the priests imagined that folk needed to be "washed down" before their goodness could again shine through. They engaged in an elaborate system of ceremonial washings and sacrifices to "make things right."

Jesus antagonized these priests by pointing out that the rituals, intended to restore a sense of goodness, backfired. All the sacrifices and washings made people feel inferior, not clean. People imagined their mistakes rendered them worthless.

The Law of Moses states that God gave these rituals. Humanity at the time could only accept a limited level of insight. Our God self only gave us what, in our mistaken view of our humanity, we thought we needed. As the letter to the Hebrews makes clear, "Sacrifice and offering You did not desire," and, "In burn offering and sacrifices for sin You had no pleasure." The negativity toward humanity codified in the priests' laws was not originally intended by God but was a reflection of the priests' own inability to believe in themselves. We felt we were inferior, and these laws reinforced our self-perception. The religious rules and rituals that grew out of the self-perception were there to reinforce our sense of unworthiness. Deep within we knew that this approach would fail and propel us to discover our true most beautiful essence.

Jesus knew that although our essentially good selves are layered over with dysfunctional behavior, this doesn't undo our fundamental goodness. We all fall short of the ideal. Our mistake is to equate our true selves with the tarnish that has dulled the silver. When we cease focusing on the tarnish, we begin to manifest the silver.

Far from focusing on people's weaknesses, Jesus simply saw beyond them. He elevated individuals above their failures, restoring their ability to believe in their innate goodness. The Christ in him never lost sight of the silver beneath the tarnish.

6

HOW CAN WE BE CHRIST-LIKE WHEN WE ARE SO OBVIOUSLY FLAWED?

—

"You're just *grouchy*," Paul's wife told him.

"I know," he responded. "But I can't stop worrying and fretting. And when I do, I cannot *not* be grouchy. They go hand in hand with me."

In this small example, Paul reminds us of ourselves. We so often say things that hurt people. We blow our top. We find ourselves becoming jealous or controlling. In lots and lots of ways, we indulge in selfish and hurtful behavior. We "forget" to disclose income from the rental apartment in the basement on our tax return; we put our work before our family for ego satisfaction; we silently take some delight in our coworkers' mistakes; we make assumptions, spread gossip, and thereby cause emotional pain to our next door neighbor.

When we see ourselves act in such ways, our tendency is to conclude that we are quite pathetic. At times like these it's easy to lose sight of our divine nature.

That we make mistakes, blow it, or are weak doesn't change the fact we are extensions and embodiments of the divine. Our mistaken self-judgment and resulting behavior flaws may mask or cloud our divinity, but they can never diminish it.

Faith is believing in your worth despite your behavior at times. It's to believe in yourself because God's own essence is *your* essence.

FEELING UNWORTHY IS OUR ORIGINAL SIN

A close reading of the second creation story in Genesis, the story of the Garden of Eden, reveals something quite different from a simple decision on the part of Adam and Eve to rebel against God. It teaches that our choices reflect what we believe about ourselves.

It's written that God had put a serpent in the garden, and this serpent persuaded Eve that God had an ulterior motive for forbidding humans to eat the fruit of the tree of the knowledge of good and evil. Though Adam and Eve were God's offspring, the serpent suggested that humans were somehow *less* than God. If they wanted to live forever like God, then they needed to *become* God-like. Eating the fruit, the serpent assured them, would endow them with the wisdom necessary to bring them up to par with God.

According to this story, evil entered the world because the serpent convinced the first humans to *doubt their adequacy*. They perceived themselves as *not good enough*. This is why they reached for the forbidden fruit. They saw it as a tree to be "desired to *make* them wise." They believed they were lacking.

Adam and Eve's fall was a fall into *disbelief in themselves*. As beings created after the "God kind," they had divine worth and all they needed to do was believe this. Had they trusted God's pronouncement that they were *already* in the divine image and therefore "very good," they would never have felt a need for the fruit of the tree of knowledge of good and evil. Instead the serpent got them to doubt their worth. It was their lack of faith in themselves that was sin.

Paradoxically, the very thing people tend to hold onto—being self-effacing, self-doubting, self-deprecating—is, according to this creation story, the root of evil! Just as the serpent talked Adam and Eve out of believing they were okay, the world in which we grow up talks us into believing we are less than we really are. Then we begin behaving in an inferior manner, well below our spiritual capacity.

Our sin doesn't lie in believing in human greatness. It lies in our *failure* to believe in ourselves.

YOUR SUPPRESSED TRUE IDENTITY

Contrary to what Christendom proposes, we don't begin life alienated from God. Jesus said it plainly: "Let the little children come to Me, and do not forbid them; for *of such is the kingdom of God.*" On the other hand, he explained that adults need to become like little children again, or they can't experience the kingdom. In other words, to be God-like comes naturally to little children.

"Original sin" is not something with which we come into the world, but something with which we are infected almost from the moment we are born. The culture teaches us to doubt ourselves, leaving us with feelings of inadequacy that we then mask with ego—a false and limited picture of ourselves. It's this systematic societal suppression of our true selves that should be labeled "original sin." It is "original" in the sense that it is a societal condition into which we are born, and which then becomes our personal mindset affecting everything we do. It is a state of self-doubt.

Not believing in ourselves is what leads us astray. *Not* valuing, accepting, and loving ourselves is our original sin, giving rise to all other evils.

Jesus confirmed this diagnosis when he said, "For from within, out of the heart of men, proceed evil thoughts" and all the actions that accompany them. In that era, they had a very different understanding of the heart. They imagined the heart to be the source of thought. Today we know that thought arises in the brain. In order to make sense of Jesus' words, we need to replace the word "heart" with "mind." Evil springs from *the way people learn to think and feel about themselves.*

The prophet Jeremiah said long ago, "The heart is deceitful above all things, and desperately wicked." Our minds play tricks on us. We fall into destructive patterns of behavior because our thoughts fool us into believing we are less than the glorious beings we really are.

Not believing in yourself undermines your goodness. Failing to delight in yourself causes your behavior to turn rogue. Putting yourself down gives rise to evil.

In its essence, sin is about holding back from totally embracing yourself and your life. It's resisting your deepest self, which longs to embrace every aspect of your life without reservation.

To be is good, and to be who you are is good. To feel yourself to be good is to assent to the truth about yourself. Sin is to go against this sense that you are good, to deny you are good. This we all learn to do in childhood.

SEE YOURSELF THROUGH NEW EYES

The lack of good feeling about ourselves that we all suffer from isn't about our character or capabilities. It's not a question of whether we are a decent person, a good citizen. If it were, all it would take to pick our spirits up would be for others to reassure us, in the way that therapists do.

The anxiety we all feel about ourselves is a fundamental anxiety about *who we are*. It goes deeper than doubting our abilities. It's the sense that *to be ourselves just isn't good enough*.

It's this deep uneasiness about ourselves that stops us from really believing in ourselves in the way Jesus believed in himself. Whereas he thoroughly enjoyed who he was, we are less than excited about being the individuals we find ourselves to be. While he felt terrific about himself, only rarely do we capture a glimpse of ourselves as delightful.

Because Jesus had broken free by not allowing the cycle of each generation to pass its shortcomings onto him, his life became a vehicle for freeing others. Something in those who allowed themselves to become close to him resonated with his essence, and they came alive in a way they hadn't been since they were children.

7

HOW DO YOU FEEL
ABOUT YOURSELF?

—

You probably flinch at the thought of discovering God within yourself, especially if you've been taught that there's nothing good about you. Didn't Paul, writing to the people of Rome, say of himself, "In my flesh dwells no good thing?"

Yes, Paul did indeed say this. But it's important to notice exactly how he worded it. He wrote to the people in Rome, "For I know that in me (that is, *in my flesh*) nothing good dwells; for *to will is present with me*, but *how to perform* what is good I do not find. For *the good that I will to do*, I do not do; but the evil *I will not to do*, that I practice."

Paul's essence wasn't evil at all. In his essence—his spirit—he longed to do good. But at this stage of his spiritual journey, he didn't know how to manifest the divine presence that was his essence. His "flesh" got in the way.

WHAT PAUL MEANT BY "FLESH"

Over the centuries, what Paul meant by flesh has been distorted. We tend to think of the body and its appetites as the "flesh." This is entirely wrong, for it puts God, who made our bodies, in conflict with what God created. In fact, scripture says we are to *cherish* our physical bodies because they are *the temple of God*.

The term "flesh" doesn't mean your body. Paul used the word *sarx* for flesh, not *soma* which means body. (We still use the term "somatic" to refer to the body.) There is no good part or bad part of a person—no part that is spiritual as opposed to a part that is unspiritual. Rather, the issue is how we *see* ourselves, and the actions that flow or fail to flow from whatever view we have of ourselves.

"Flesh" in Paul's way of thinking is a state of *mind*. He calls it the "carnal mind"—"carnal" means flesh. This is your mind in its usual state of anxious thought and emotional reactivity, cut off from your divine essence. It's you encumbered by all the things you tell yourself, instead of flowing from your spirit, which is your center. It's you when you don't allow your spirit, which is one with the divine, to guide your life.

Your essence is different from the person you may have thought you are. This is why Jesus said you have to lose what you think of as "your life" in order to *truly* find your life.

The deepest part of you is good and seeks to do good. As Paul found, at heart he wanted to do the right thing even though his thought-plagued, emotionally-reactive mind got in the way. In his essence he determined to do good. So much so that, whenever he failed to do what he intended to do, he concluded, "It's no longer I who do it, but sin *that dwells in me.*"

The real Paul knew he was good! It was only his turbulent carnal mind that spoiled everything. Of course! How could he not be essentially good? His essence was divine. As happened with Jesus, as his belief in his true identity increased, his life began to bear the imprint of the divine likeness that the Hebrew spiritual tradition had long said is our human heritage.

Like Paul, you and I experience a war going on within ourselves. We do things we know better than to do, and we resist doing things we truly ought to do.

In our struggle to be who we really long to be, we have someone to look to for encouragement. Says the letter to the Hebrews, Jesus experienced this same struggle. It's a struggle he won because at all times he maintained a clear sense of who he was—of his deeper self, his essence, his spirit.

It's to your deeper being, your true self, that Jesus appeals. He seeks to awaken in you who you have always been in essence.

FIGHT THE GOOD FIGHT OF FAITH

Perhaps you are like many of us who, in our more honest moments, realize we don't experience the glorious life Jesus promised. You try hard, but much of the time you feel more like a failure than a reflection of God.

As long as you really don't *believe* the good news of who you are as a part of the Christ—as long as you are plagued with doubt about yourself—you can't possibly experience the power of the divine nature at work in you. This is why Paul urged, "Fight the good fight of *faith.*"

The battle isn't to try to do the right thing. It's to *see yourself as Jesus saw himself.* When you see yourself in this way, doing the right thing happens spontaneously. There's no struggle because all the good you accomplish flows from your enjoyment of the restful state of the promised land.

The only struggle—the only battle—is one of faith versus self-doubt.

The good news Jesus proclaimed is the opposite of the self-doubt that's so widespread in those who are supposed to be people of faith. For Jesus, to have faith is to believe in your essential divinity.

We are all *evolving* into the recognition of who we really are. In fact, it's because we don't automatically see who we are that Jesus was crucified. He died to show us the evolution that has yet to occur in us, for which the Bible uses the term "sin"—falling short of our potential to manifest the Christ.

Everything we are ashamed of in our lives finds its origin in not feeling good about ourselves, not believing in ourselves.

WHY BELIEVE IN YOURSELF?

But aren't you supposed to trust in God, not in yourself?

To believe in yourself *apart* from God would be no different from pulling yourself up by your own bootstraps. This can be learned on the therapist's couch. Faith is different. Faith is to believe in yourself *in* God.

For a time Paul also struggled to see himself as he really was in his Christ essence. What he called "the old man," his lifelong habit of seeing himself as inferior, dogged his steps for a while. At one point he even cried out, "Wretched man that I am!"

I can identify with what Paul was feeling, can't you? How many times have I allowed myself to be taken over by the reactionary part of the brain we share with reptiles! Like a snake that strikes or an alligator that snaps when threatened, I would react instead of thinking before I opened my mouth. Paul, too, knew all-too-well how easy it is to *lose* your head instead of *using* it.

How did Paul get out of this deadly trap? He explained, "I thank God—through Jesus Christ our Lord!" He stepped out of the tyranny of his thoughts and emotions and began functioning from the Christ nature that had always been his essence.

Paul learned to bring "every thought into captivity" to the Christ nature at his center. He called this living "according to the spirit" instead of "according to the flesh." His reptilian brain no longer ruled him. Rather, he learned to "reign in life" with Christ, so that his bodily existence was directed by his divine essence instead of from his egoic thoughts and emotional reactivity.

The key, says Paul, is to "reckon," or consider, your old self dead. To "reckon" doesn't mean to *imagine* your old self dead. Rather, it's coming to terms with what's true, even though you can't quite appreciate it yet. You choose to believe what's real, not the habitual thought patterns of your mind.

Think back to my experience of learning to drive on the right hand side of the road. When I made a mistake, it would have been foolish to tell myself I was still in England. Just as illogically, many of us tell ourselves God can't possibly live in us because sometimes we act in ways that are unloving.

The fact is, once you become aware of your Christ essence, you are no longer the same person. Before, you lived from your thoughts and emotions, as if you didn't even have a spiritual dimension. Even many churchgoers simply don't know they have a spiritual essence. But once you realize that you are essentially spirit, you don't see yourself the same way again.

The old really deceases. It's no longer you, as you have always thought of yourself, who is living. The Christ lives *as* you.

8

JESUS OPENS
OUR EYES

—

Seeing into Jesus, you see *yourself*. In him, you know yourself for the first time. Your race, color, culture, class, and sex no longer define you. You understand yourself to be precious not because you are a certain gender, or because you come from a certain family or were born in a certain nation, but because you are *an expression of God's own being*.

We don't automatically see God in ourselves. Writing to the Corinthians, Paul explains that our natural senses are tuned to the material world and aren't normally aware of God's presence. This is why, when we try to imagine God, we end up creating merely a human projection.

"No one knows the things of God except the Spirit of God," Paul says. Before we can experience God within us, we must "receive" the spirit.

UNDERSTANDING SPIRIT

When you hear that you need to "receive" the spirit, perhaps you assume it means you were empty and God had to give you the spirit. You didn't have it, and now you do.

But spirit isn't a substance, a sort of ether. It isn't any kind of "thing." Hence it isn't an ingredient that must be inserted into your humanity. When you receive the spirit, nothing is *added* to you.

Notice carefully what Paul told the Corinthians about spirit. He equated spirit with "knowing." Spirit is consciousness. The Holy Spirit is divine consciousness.

To receive the Spirit of God is to have our God-consciousness activated.

If you tell a friend something about herself that she is unaware of, she may or may not receive it. If she doesn't receive it, it doesn't make it any less true. She simply doesn't "get" what you are saying—doesn't see herself as she really is.

To receive the spirit is to have our eyes opened to something that has always been true of us. In the words of Peter in one of his New Testament letters, we become aware that we, like Jesus, are "partakers of the divine nature."

The divine nature wasn't an *ingredient* in the mind of Jesus. Rather, Jesus participated in God's being, *as we all do*—although it may be difficult for some of us to "receive" this truth.

SPIRIT ENABLES US TO SEE WHAT MATTERS

The letter to the Ephesians says that only when "the eyes of your understanding" are *"enlightened"* do you experience God's presence within you. The metaphor of enlightenment is used often in the New Testament. Enlightenment means "to receive insight," that is, inward sight. You finally see something that's always been true of you.

The coming of the spirit is likened not only to having our eyes opened, but also to having our blindness lifted, receiving our sight, and being delivered out of darkness into light. We grow up with our understanding darkened by the influence of society, robbed of insight into who we truly are.

It's in this sense that we are "of the world." Our attention is directed everywhere but where it really needs to be, which shortchanges us of our enjoyment of life. We dedicate ourselves to things we've been taught are important but that don't reflect our essential being. Once our focus shifts from the external world to our internal being, we finally see what really matters. This is the experience of the coming of the spirit, which frees us from the mesmerizing influences of the world.

Curing our alienation from God doesn't require that a different nature be imparted to us. Paul described the human condition clearly: "Having their *understanding darkened*, being alienated from the life of God, *because of the ignorance that is in them*, because of the blindness of their heart." Our problem is that we don't know ourselves, don't see ourselves, and therefore lose ourselves to the influence of other people.

Receiving the spirit isn't a joining of humanity to divinity. *It's recognizing that human being and divine being are fundamentally the same.* To "receive" the spirit is to become conscious of this.

Jesus' followers talked repeatedly of being "filled" with the spirit. To be filled with the spirit is to have a *continual* awareness of God's presence within you—as you.

Similarly, to be filled with love isn't to be filled up with an ingredient of some sort. Love isn't a substance that's poured into us. It's a permanent state of our being. So too are joy and peace.

Filled with the spirit, you are no longer driven by your biological urges, emotional reactions, and selfishness. Everything you do is a reflection of your loving, peaceful essence, which harnesses every facet of your body and soul for the purpose of good.

9

ENJOY WHO YOU ARE

—

Jesus said, "Follow me."

At first glance this hardly sounds like an invitation to be yourself. In fact, for 2,000 years, millions have harbored the secret fear, "If I follow Jesus, I'm not going to get to do what I really want to do. Even worse, if I follow Jesus, life is going to be hard. I won't have much fun because I'll have to give up a lot of things. After all, didn't Jesus say, 'Deny yourself, take up your cross, and follow me?' That sounds like suffering. I'm afraid of suffering. Why can't I just enjoy my life?"

These were the thoughts a young woman confided when, at the end of her sophomore year at college, she came to talk to me about her future. She was torn between wanting to be like Jesus and wanting a fulfilling life.

"If you really want a fulfilling life, you need to discover your divine purpose," I told her.

"If you mean I need to discover God's *will* for me, that frightens me," she confessed.

I took a sip of tea, then sat back in my chair. "You're afraid of what God might ask you to do?"

She sighed. "It's bound to be the opposite of what I really want to do."

I set my teacup down, looked into her eyes, and meeting her at her current level of understanding, I said, "I think God's will is always exactly what we really want to do. This is what Jesus tried to get people to understand."

She looked confused. "But I thought Jesus said that to follow him, we have to deny ourselves."

"That's true," I said. "But Jesus wasn't talking about giving up the things you are passionate about. For Jesus, doing the will of God meant being himself in the fullest sense, doing *exactly* what he wanted to do."

She still looked puzzled, so I continued, "To follow Jesus isn't an invitation to copy the life of a Jewish carpenter and teacher in ancient Palestine, trying to play the role he played. Rather, it's to become the *kind* of person he was, a person guided by the presence of God within. This means learning to be your true self, which is an expression of God's image in you."

I could almost see the wheels turning in this young lady's head as she mulled over what I had said. A glint of hope appeared in her eyes. The thought of being able to be herself was clearly encouraging. Then self-doubt reasserted itself and she protested, "But aren't we supposed to sacrifice? What about Jesus' command to 'take up our cross daily'?"

I smiled. "There'll be plenty of sacrificing once you discover what your life's mission is. But this kind of sacrifice doesn't deprive you of what you want out of life. On the contrary, it enables you to achieve it. You'll willingly spend yourself for what you're meant to do. The more you give yourself to something you truly love, the greater your fulfillment. Jesus gave everything—his life. His death was the price he paid to accomplish what he wanted to do. He was being his true self, and that's why he did it without reservation."

GOD INVITES YOU TO BE YOURSELF

Jesus presents us with a paradox. On the one hand, the gospel writers reveal a man who was fully himself. On the other, they make it clear that Jesus was obedient to God in every aspect of his life. Isn't being yourself a contradiction to being obedient to God?

Jesus' understanding of the will of the Father is different from how many think of God's will, which is generally understood as contrary to our desires. Like it was to the young woman mentioned earlier, to many, to obey God's will seems a chore that requires giving up what they really want to do.

We have trouble with this word "obey" today. Obedience is a concept that comes from an era that was more authoritarian than our democratic era. In that patriarchal world, kings decreed, husbands lorded it over wives, and children were to be seen and not heard.

Even the "will" of God sounds like an *imposition* rather than an *invitation*.

The New Testament authors spoke of God as a king and a lord not because God is a king or a lord, but because they were restricted to the language of their day and bound by the images of their world. Theirs was an era of kings and lords, so it was these images they borrowed to speak of what was most essential in their lives. To understand the "will" of God and what it means to be "obedient" to God, it's necessary to shed the authoritarian overtones of the language.

The good news Jesus proclaimed is characterized by *invitation*. It's helpful to switch to the language Jesus began to introduce just before his death, as he spoke of his followers as "friends" instead of servants. He stressed that love—a *passion* for life and for people, not just "obediently" toeing the line—is the mark of doing the will of God.

This is why Jesus' death—a willing step he took that was absolutely true to who he was—is called his passion. What you are passionate about, not in your head and thoughts, but in your heart and spirit, is where God's will is found.

GOD'S COMMANDS ARE INTERNAL

Once we get away from its authoritarian connotations, we discover that the sense in which God "commands" our obedience is quite different from the commands of a tyrannical ruler. It comes out in Jesus' use of the word "commandment" when he said to his disciples, "This is My commandment, that you love one another as I have loved you." There's nothing authoritarian in this statement.

Rather, Jesus is asking us to pay attention to something to which we tend not to pay attention, our loving essence. (How to do this will be addressed in Chapter 25.) It's a command that's only necessary because we've been conditioned to be inattentive. Jesus was saying, "Be the loving person you now are." It's like a command to practice the violin. To a child who doesn't want to learn the violin this would be torture. To someone just hired to play in an orchestra, it's a joy.

As Paul explained to the Corinthians, instead of being written in a book with pen and ink like the laws of Moses, or engraved on tablets of stone like the ten commandments, God's commands are inscribed on the human heart. God's will is an *internal impulse*, not an external demand. It's your deep longing—perhaps suppressed for years—to be the unique person you alone can be.

God's commandments are your heart's intuition.

The author of Hebrews affirms that God's commands are readily found in the human heart and mind: "I will put My laws in their mind and write them on their hearts."

Paul likewise told the Romans that, once you understand that God is within you, no great effort is needed to find the divine will. It comes naturally, springing *spontaneously* into your thoughts and words. God's commands are the voice of your true self. To obey God is to be obedient to your most heartfelt desires.

There's nothing arbitrary about God's will. God doesn't ask of you things that contradict what you really want. The will of God eclipses neither human reason nor human desire. Rather, it enlivens both. It raises them up to the transcendent level of your Christ self, which is the source of all reason and all desire.

Faith becomes the launching pad for a life empowered by both reason and passion. It denies neither, yet goes beyond them with a wholeness that integrates every part of us.

We know we are true to ourselves when every part of us is fully alive.

JESUS WAS COMPLETELY HIMSELF

In Paul's letter to the Philippians, Jesus is said to have been "obedient even to the point of death." This doesn't merely mean that Jesus stuck it out to the bitter end. A shallow reading of this has led people to believe that Jesus went against everything in him that wanted to live. We assume he did the opposite of what he really wanted to do, but that he was willing to do it because God required it of him.

But Jesus' death wasn't something God forced on him. His obedience wasn't passive resignation to what God asked of him. It wasn't a matter of gritting his teeth, going through with something that inwardly he resisted all the way.

The outstanding thing about Jesus was his willingness to grow to the point that he was capable of *total* obedience to the divine self at his center, even to the point of death.

In going to his death, Jesus was acting in freedom. He stated emphatically that no one took his life from him, he laid it down of his own choice. In other words, his ability to be himself without any inhibition—to be the person he knew himself to be without apology—propelled him to *embrace his own death*.

Jesus had taught others, "If the Son makes you free, you will be free indeed." In overcoming his own fear and allowing himself to undergo an agonizing death, Jesus was acting in total freedom and with complete integrity.

To be obedient to God is to respond to the desire within us that seeks to stretch us to our potential. We hanker for this freedom, yet shrink from it. This is natural. In the Garden of Gethsemane on the eve of his crucifixion, Jesus also shrank from ultimate freedom as he prayed repeatedly, "If it is possible, let this cup pass from me." But despite his momentary horror at the ordeal facing him, he embraced death as the climax of his God-inspired life. God's will and his will were identical. In going to the cross, he was following the same inner voice that had guided him all along.

Have you ever said, "I need to obey my heart?" This is the sense in which Jesus obeyed God. He was following an impulse that emerged from his certainty of who he was and what the fulfillment of his purpose entailed.

The image of Jesus willingly allowing himself to be crucified burns into our souls the huge difference between how a person who knows himself to be one with God acts, and how people who don't have an awareness of their oneness with God act. When you own your Christ nature, you know there is nothing to fear in being true to yourself to the nth degree.

Even though leaving home to become a leader of men and women would end in his death, Jesus "for the *joy* that was set before him, endured the cross," disregarding its shame. Because he was doing what he loved doing, he gave his life for what he believed in.

When you are in touch with your true desires, you give yourself joyfully to life. Because you are doing what you love to do, commitment and dedication flow naturally.

By being your true self, you have something worthwhile to contribute. Serving isn't experienced as an obligation, but as an extension of your own sense of competence. "Sacrificing"—to make sacred by extending your loving essence—is a joyous expression of yourself.

10

EVERYTHING YOU HAVE EVER LONGED FOR

—

Beneath the brave face we like to put on life, within the hearts of many of us is a profound feeling of disappointment. It's not disappointment over any particular thing. We can generally get over the ways we have been hurt. If we can't do it alone, we find a friend, a minister, or a therapist. This disappointment goes much deeper.

"Time heals all wounds," we say.

Yet there is a woundedness that isn't touched by the passing of years. Unlike the many hurts from which we recover, this is a sense of disappointment over life itself. It's a pain that doesn't go away.

This pain shows up as a sadness, a yearning, a bewildering discontentment, a feeling of emptiness—and you don't even know where it comes from.

Jesus described this longing as a "thirst" we are unable to quench.

GETTING PAST DISAPPOINTMENT

Traveling from Galilee to Jerusalem, a route that took him through Samaria, Jesus arrived at a fork in the road. It was high noon. Tired from the heat and the journey, he sat down by a well. A Samaritan woman soon approached the well from the village of Sychar.

It was uncommon for anyone to draw water in the heat of the day.

It was also unusual for the woman to be drawing water from this particular well because there was a well in Sychar.

The woman had been married five times. With so many failed marriages, and her hopes pinned on a sixth man with whom she was living, her life was a mess, and she felt alienated from her community. Instead of filling her bucket in the village with the other women at the evening water drawing, she slunk off to this isolated well more than half a mile away during the heat of high noon when nobody was around.

Jesus asked the woman to give him a drink. The woman was surprised. "How is it that you, being a Jew, ask a drink of me, a Samaritan woman?" she queried. Jews didn't normally speak to Samaritans because they considered them to have forsaken their faith.

Jesus responded that if the woman had known who was asking her for a drink, she would have asked him to give *her* a drink, and he would have given her "living water."

Jesus' strange response intrigued the woman. Where would he get water, since he had no bucket?

Many translations miss the richness of the story because they translate two different Greek words with the one English word "well." When the woman spoke of the well, she used a word that meant a deep well with still water. But when Jesus spoke of the well, he used a word that meant a spring with flowing, sparkling water.

Water symbolizes life. When you drink from a well, you get thirsty again. "But whoever drinks of the water that I shall give him will never thirst," Jesus explained. "But the water that I shall give him will become in him a fountain of water springing up into everlasting life."

While drawing from the well pictured the effort of merely getting by each day that characterized the woman's life, a spring symbolized Jesus' experience of an abiding fullness of life. For the woman, life was burdensome—like the repeated drudgery of drawing water just to survive each day. In contrast, Jesus had an ecstatic sense of himself that simply bubbled up within him.

As they talked, the woman realized Jesus could see the emptiness of her life. He knew the disappointment she felt from her failed marriages. Hurt, loneliness, and longing were written all over her.

Letting down her guard, the woman allowed Jesus to show her that her emptiness wasn't the *result* of her failed relationships—it was the *cause*. Though each new partner quenched her thirst for a time, she soon felt parched again and had to drop her bucket back into the well.

It was because the woman didn't know her true self that she couldn't connect with anyone in a meaningful way. Unhappy with herself, she sought happiness in men.

WHAT WE ALL LONG FOR

The portrait of the Samaritan woman mirrors the deep hurt in all our lives. Her search for happiness reflects our own search for happiness. Her longing for fulfillment speaks to our own longing for fulfillment.

We imagine that we long for a particular person, job, or other external reality. While getting what we think we want sedates our pain for a while, it doesn't eliminate it. Like the Samaritan woman, we usually have to chase an elusive happiness down many dead end paths before we realize that nothing satisfies us for long. We continue to feel restless, anxious, unfulfilled.

Jesus shows us our longing in a new light. Our longing isn't for something we don't have. *It's for a self we have lost touch with.*

Jesus' response to the Samaritan woman's plight was to make her aware of her own potential for experiencing the fullness of life. Happiness was not something to be found on the outside. It was within her, if she but knew it.

If you try to get your needs met through another person, you eventually meet up with disappointment. You discover that there is a sense in which you are still alone. Your partner can't always "be there" for you. Having a partner doesn't bring you the complete feeling of fulfillment for which you yearn or the deep joy for which you hunger. Something is still missing.

When you find that your partner isn't meeting your needs, like the Samaritan woman, you may try a different partner. In time you find that this person can't meet all your needs either.

When you make the painful discovery that no one can be every-thing you want, you are primed for the realization that your partner was never meant to meet your needs! Only *you* can meet your needs through accepting your oneness with God. It's this that heals the sep-aration and ends loneliness.

The various people, things, and situations that make up our lives can never be the source of our fulfillment. Chasing after all of these eventually teaches us this, as it taught the Samaritan woman. She learned the lesson Jesus illustrates in the parable of the prodigal son—that we have to come "home" to *ourselves* in order to find fulfillment.

BEING YOURSELF LEADS TO CONNECTION

Jesus speaks of "giving" the Samaritan woman the soul-quenching water for which she longed. It's evident that Jesus didn't give some "thing" to the woman, as if spirit were a substance. We are in a world of metaphor, with water as a symbol of the divine life that longs to bubble up within us.

What Jesus imparted to the woman was the gift of insight. "He told me everything I ever did," she reported to her neighbors. Jesus enabled her to make sense of her five failed marriages by sharing with her an understanding of what had gone wrong in her life to cause her to lose touch with her real self. In this way he gave her the water of life that never runs dry.

When the woman got in touch with her essence through the insight Jesus imparted to her, she realized she wasn't her past behav-ior. She had within her all the resources she needed for a truly fulfill-ing life. As a result, her relationships with everybody changed. Because she had become her own answer to her longing, she no longer looked to relationships for fulfillment. This enabled her to love people unconditionally, which so amazed the people of her village that they too came to meet Jesus. Because of the woman's experience, the whole village connected with each other at a new level.

To varying degrees, all of us have been crippled in our ability to realize our Christ self. This not only limits us individually, it limits our experience of oneness. When we step into the Christ nature, we are healed both individually and collectively. We become truly ourselves, while also including others in deep communion.

From birth, to different degrees we breathe in the foul air of disconnectedness, alienation, and hostility. Our divine potential to be true to ourselves, and from this deep appreciation for ourselves connect deeply with others, is eclipsed. Pretty soon we are living in a manner that totally masks our real nature. We crush the part of us that is capable of the connection Jesus had with people by rejecting the divine self in which we ought to delight.

The woman's transformation entailed realizing that her whole life had been driven by a search for a self that had been lost. When she found her real self, it became a spring within her that welled up into a fulfilled life.

What we all really long for is to be *ourselves* in the fullest sense, while also connecting at a profound level with others. This is why Jesus introduces us to the kingdom of God as a family. It's not about individualism—it's about community. The second coming of Christ is the realization of a global community of people who know themselves to be part of the corporate spiritual body we know as the Christ.

At your center is a fullness that longs to express itself. This fullness is the Infinite seeking to manifest itself through your human form. You are not empty, needing to be filled. You are *a fullness of potential seeking to come fully alive.*

This fullness isn't simply a ticket to enjoying life. It's meant to be shared. The Infinite seeks to express itself through you by inviting you to become ever more sharply defined as an individual, yet ever more closely connected in oneness. Realizing that you are not empty, but full, enables you to establish the kind of fulfilling relationships that someday will characterize how the entire world relates.

11

WHAT DO YOU REALLY WANT?

—

"Ask what you desire," Jesus said. Was he saying that you can dream up anything you feel like, and hey presto, it will be yours?

"Ask, and it will be given you," he also said, "seek, and you will find; knock, and it will be opened to you." But he made it clear that he wasn't just talking about your basic needs, such as your bodily requirements. As he explained, "Your heavenly father knows you need all these things."

Jesus also wasn't talking about only asking for material goods. He knew that no matter how many things you acquire, they can't fulfill you. When he said ask for what you desire, he was speaking of your heart's desire. Beyond your everyday survival needs, Jesus wanted you to discover what in your heart you truly *want*.

In the view of Jesus, desire in its essence is *spiritual*. When he used the term "want," he was speaking of desire in the sense of what you *enjoy*. We're talking about enjoying your essential self, not merely enjoyment of the surface things humans tend to spend their lives chasing after.

Jesus came so that we "may have life," and that we "may have it more abundantly." If life is lived abundantly, it should bring a great deal of enjoyment.

To live is to enjoy, not just endure. Enjoying is what makes life abundant. Indeed, the most intimate, most "me" thing about each of us is the form our desire takes—our particular likes and dislikes. One loves to cook, another crafts fine furniture, and yet another paints.

Enjoying yourself is often frowned upon, especially by the religious, as if you shouldn't enjoy yourself "too much." Many live by the maxim that we are supposed to be satisfied with what we really need.

But abundant life doesn't mean just getting by. Jesus wished more for us than "I'm okay" or "Have a nice day." He said life can be so fulfilling that it's *packed* with good feeling—"good measure, pressed down, shaken together, and running over."

RETHINKING DESIRE

Desire isn't needy. Contrary to what almost everyone believes, desire flows in the opposite direction from need.

We get confused about this because we use the words "desire" and "want" in two different ways. Sometimes we are referring to what we don't have but wish we had. This is the kind of wanting that the Buddha recognized leads to grief. It's craving, clinging, being needy. The more authentic meaning of desire is found in enjoying something—really wanting it in the sense of *relishing* it.

Desire as a spiritual experience is *cherishing* someone or something.

Relationships are a good illustration of the difference between these two uses of the word "want." Too often couples really want each other in the sense of craving each other before they get married. But once they marry, they no longer want each other with the same passion.

In most marriages there's *far too little* desire between partners! How many couples have one foot in and one foot out of their commitment to each other? Christian marriages are no exception. There's an amazing absence of passion, even an abhorrence of passion, in the people of the Passion.

When you are in touch with your essence, you're not needy. Your center isn't a vacuum that seeks to suck the world into it. Far from being empty with little to give, you have infinite resources within you.

Desire thought of as an emptiness yearning to be filled produces the grasping attachment that's a source of heartache. Desire experienced as a fullness seeking to be expressed leads to an ecstatic feeling of fulfillment—abundant life.

The entire universe has come into existence out of the fullness of the Creator's own essence, which is compelled to express itself. The cosmos is God's desire for self-expression fulfilled.

Desire flows out of a sense of your own fullness. It's wanting to experience the fullness at your center, a fullness that's been dammed up.

DO YOU ALWAYS KNOW WHAT YOU WANT?

Instinct leads animals to what they want. But in humans, desire is added to instinct.

Because we often don't know what we really want, desire frequently takes a roundabout route through a jungle of whims. Discovering desire as a fullness seeking to be expressed means learning to distinguish what you *really* want from your whims. How often have you pursued people, things, and experiences you imagined would make your life full and exciting, only to discover that you were craving something you didn't really want once you got it?

Often only by chasing what you *think* you want do you eventually—and usually painfully—discover the difference between your needs, your whims, and your true *desires*.

This equips you to take care of your needs, be wary of your whims, and pay close attention to your heartfelt desires.

Your desires emanate from your essential being. Fulfillment at home, work, and play necessitates getting in touch with these desires and bringing them to bear on your daily life. You must become clear about what you really want.

Becoming clear about what you want isn't always easy and takes getting quiet. You enter the stillness, and allow yourself to feel what emerges. When you become aware of what truly matters to you, you focus your attention on this and allow yourself to become intentional about inviting it into your life. As Jesus said, you have to "seek" until you find and "knock" until the door opens. You seek by entering the stillness, and you knock by forming your intention and pursuing it.

When Jesus said that you need to go after what you truly want, he also gave us the key to making it happen. You will have what you truly want, he promised, "if you abide in Me, and My words abide in you." To abide in Jesus is to stay in our Christ self. To allow his words to abide in us is to pay attention to the creative insights that come to us from within, then adopt them. If we are in tune with our Christ essence, our desires will be fulfilled. They will be fulfilled because *we will be guided to fulfill them.*

Since creating is the fundamental God action, when we abide in our Christ nature we connect with the womb of potentiality. Creative insights will then naturally bubble up within us daily. It's from these insights that we then set our intentions to create. When these insights come, they reflect our heart's true desires. We can rely on these. Approaching our lives from this place, nothing is denied us. We will be prompted when to act. Then we need only witness the manifestation. There's no struggle, no agonizing.

When you follow those pursuits that reflect your interests, every dimension of your life flows from your heart. This is what makes each day meaningful. It's the key to living a fulfilling life.

PRISONERS OF OUR YEARNING FOR SECURITY

Most humans sell themselves short. They settle. Given life's pressures, it's easy to become preoccupied with frantically trying to take care of immediate needs.

A friend of mine settles for a relationship that isn't fulfilling because she's tired of being alone. A man I know does a job he hates, but he stays because it pays well. He was always told that security should be his primary concern.

Sometimes intermediate steps are necessary, especially when the wolf is at the door. But as long as we are focused only on meeting basic needs, we avoid diving beneath the surface to our heartfelt desires, which alone can bring us fulfillment.

Some people have the courage to change course when they realize their lives are out of step with their real desires. As an example, one man grew up to be an attorney because his father was an attorney. But he never really enjoyed the work. When he was hired by a large corporation, he felt out of his depth and found himself battling feelings of incompetence. Eventually, against his father's advice, he quit and went back to school. It was a difficult and costly decision. Years later, as an accountant, he felt both competent and satisfied. "Figures are my thing," he told his father. "They come easily to me."

It's difficult for many of us to follow our heart's desires because we try to do the prudent thing and put security first. But Jesus emphasized discovering what you *really* want—and then going after it.

BLESS PEOPLE WITH YOUR UNIQUENESS

In Jesus, this was already happening at a remarkably young age. By the time he was twelve, he had such a strong sense of his divine essence that the first time he journeyed to Jerusalem with his parents, he went freely about the city pursuing his mission. His parents recognized his maturity and, when they began the journey home, didn't even check that he was with the caravan headed back to Nazareth.

In fact, Jesus had stayed behind in Jerusalem. It was a full day before his parents missed him. Suddenly becoming anxious, they returned to the city. And where did they find him? In the temple, surrounded by scholars who were amazed by his insights. When his parents expressed their anxiety, his response was to assure them that it was only natural for him to be in what he called "My Father's house." He was engaged in what he sensed his life was all about. Even at the age of twelve, he was busy following the guidance of the Christ nature within him.

Years later, not once do we find Jesus consulting his disciples concerning whether he was doing the right thing. He had no self-doubt, and consequently no need to seek reassurance from others. Even when the disciples protested as he embarked on his final journey to Jerusalem, he showed no wavering. This is because his certainty didn't come from others but from within him.

Jesus neither became enmeshed with others nor had to pull away from them in order to "find himself." He could be alone when he wanted to, and he could be with others, without any disturbance of his inner peace. He knew a Sabbath rest in all circumstances. Alone or among others, he was completely comfortable with himself because there was no neediness in him, no grasping. His life flowed effortlessly and spontaneously from the desiring heart of the universe, as it sought to pour itself out through him in love.

Discovering your essential self brings with it a feeling of confidence. This feeling of confidence empowers you to reach out to serve others. When you know you're good at something, you are delighted to help. Because in your essence you feel exuberantly loving, joyous, and excited, you want to extend yourself out into the world. Your life becomes a life of joyful service, a blessing to everyone around you. Desire as a spiritual experience is always self-giving. Sharing from fullness, you are fulfilled.

12

HOW FREE ARE YOU?

—

We in the West think of ourselves as free agents. To an extent we can choose the lives we wish to lead. We are free to make decisions concerning our careers, relationships, and where and how we live. But how deep does our freedom actually run?

Whenever you make a choice, it begins to define you. You are teamed with a particular person or a certain career, and this determines much about how you spend your days.

Once you are bound by a choice, you may find that the person you truly want to be doesn't emerge in the life you have selected for yourself. This sets up a tension within you. Your deepest self is trying to express itself in circumstances that restrict its expression, and you feel torn.

Fulfillment lies in committing yourself to expressing your divine essence. For this to happen, you have to become *truly* free.

UNDERSTANDING "FLESH" AND "SPIRIT"

When you don't act from your Christ nature, you live from what Jesus and Paul called the "flesh." As we saw in Chapter 7, "flesh" is a state of mind, not the physical body and its appetites. To live "according to the flesh" is to be emotionally, mentally, and spiritually fragmented. You base your behavior on a particular aspect of yourself and ignore the rest of who you are. There's a lack of balance, a failure to integrate the different aspects of your being into a wholeness.

"Flesh" is the set of attitudes you learned as a child. It's the feeling that to be yourself isn't particularly delightful. And, since you aren't all that desirable, you shouldn't want too much. You are supposed to be "humble," which people think means holding back.

As you grow up, the picture you form of yourself becomes, in your mind, who you are, *period*. You think this is *all* you are. It's a very limited view of your humanity—a view of yourself in which you are imprisoned. You come to believe that settling for mediocrity is the wise course. You convince yourself that surviving from day to day is all there is to life, all you can hope for.

Living as if life were simply a matter of having to "make the best of it" is what the New Testament calls being "worldly."

If to live "according to the flesh" is to have a narrow attitude toward life, then to live "according to the spirit" is to be your expansive divine self.

Flesh and spirit are at war, in the sense that the Infinite constantly tugs at you, seeking to break you out of your limited view of yourself. It wants you to reach with your whole being toward your potential.

This tug-of-war isn't between imagined "higher" and "lower" parts of you. It's a tension between your desire to commit yourself wholeheartedly to the adventure of life, and the tendency to succumb to inertia. A characteristic of "sin" is inertia—living a restricted life that isn't open to the divine essence as it seeks to express itself through you.

The good news of Jesus is that you don't have to stay stuck in this half-life.

SALVATION IS WHOLENESS

At your deepest level you *yearn to act with your whole being*. But the self-limiting attitudes with which you have grown up cause you to dread this ever happening. At first it's usually frightening to find the whole of yourself coming together in a "yes" to somebody or some venture.[12]

Humans are compulsive two-timers. When there's a decision facing us, we tend to leave part of ourselves out of it. We make the decision, but we always make sure there's an escape clause. If something is good for us, we still hold part of ourselves back from making a total commitment. If we suspect something isn't good for us, we nevertheless like to dabble with it. We don't like finality in our choices.

Jesus spoke of people as "perishing" and said that he came to "save" the perishing. In more modern language, we might say he came to bring wholeness to dysfunctional people. Far from being something that you experience only when you die, being "saved" involves progressively shedding your fractured sense of yourself and learning to act as a whole person.

When you bring your whole self to life, you begin to enjoy "eternal" life, sometimes translated "everlasting" life. "Eternal" isn't primarily a word that has to do with quantity, as in an endless life—though it can include this. It's more often a qualitative term. For instance, Jonah is said to have been in the belly of a great fish "forever," though he was only there three days. But while he was there, he was totally immersed in the experience. The priestly office that was part of the Law of Moses was also said to be "eternal," though it ended when it was replaced by Christ. The letter of Jude says the people of Sodom suffered the vengeance of "eternal fire," even though Jesus speaks of them being shown tolerance in the judgment, and Ezekiel describes them as ultimately living once again in their own land under a new covenant God will make with all peoples.

"Eternal" life is a life in which you are fully immersed, to the point that you are unaware of time. Because you are one-hundred percent present in whatever you are doing, time seems to stop. You embrace each and every moment as if it were the only reality there is.

The "perishing" don't bring their whole selves to life, reaping instead the consequences of the destructive patterns of behavior that come with being fractured. Because they don't live fully in the eternal "now," often they are tortured by time.

We speak of someone who has lost their way in life as a "lost soul." This is how Jesus understood being lost. His self-determined life saved his followers from their lost condition because it awakened them to their divine essence. He came to be thought of as their "savior" because he was the representative, the symbol, the embodiment of this desired yet dreaded divinity in each of us.

Jesus represents your wholeness, which beckons to you at every moment. You can only bring your whole self to life to the degree you really know yourself. Salvation is a process of self-discovery. Wholeness is a condition in which there is no more unconsciousness. Your inner being has become transparent. You are no longer driven by subconscious fears, and you no longer flee your true desires.

JESUS LIVED FROM HIS CENTER

All the spokes of Jesus' everyday existence flowed from the hub of his deepest self, which was centered in God. In every aspect of his life, he behaved in a manner in which his choices reflected his divine nature, so that his whole life came to be an expression of who he was. In a word, his life had *integrity*. His whole existence lined up with his divine being. The outer reflected the inner.

The word integrity is a modern term. In Jesus' day they said that such a person was "perfect." We think of being perfect as never making a mistake, which is foreign to its New Testament use. To speak of perfection in biblical terms is to mean that *a person could bring their whole being to every part of their life.*

The author of Hebrews tells us that Jesus had to be "perfected." He had to discover, in every aspect of his life, what it meant for his whole being to line up with his divinity. What did it mean to have integrity in terms of his work? What did it mean with respect to his mother, brothers, and sisters? What was it to behave with integrity among his closest followers, both male and female?

By the end of his life, Jesus had risen to a mature level of wholeness. He knew what it was to act with integrity in every area of his life. He could bring his whole being to all that he did. This is how he was "perfected."

Such a highly developed sense of integrity didn't come easily. As Hebrews explains, Jesus "learned obedience by the things which he suffered." In every choice he made, he had to ask himself what sort of person he was becoming. Did a particular decision expand his freedom to be true to his deepest self, or restrict it? Whatever the cost, he had to learn to choose the road that led to greater freedom.

What is it that God asks of us? What does God want from us? Nothing more than that we should act with our whole authentic being in everything we do.

13

GIVE LIFE YOUR ALL

—

To act with *all* of yourself involved, committed, is the key to fulfillment. Only when you hold nothing back does your life have integrity.

But there is a price tag for wholeness.

In the backwater Galilean village of perhaps two hundred inhabitants in which Jesus grew up, he was regarded as a nobody. When, later, he came to fame, the villagers who had known him all his life were not just surprised, they were disdainful. "Who does he think he is?" they scoffed (I am paraphrasing). "Isn't he the carpenter's son? Since when did he become a scholar?"

Their reaction was understandable in that culture. Jesus was on, or close to, the bottom rung of the social ladder. We're told that, like his father, he was a carpenter. When I think of a carpenter, I think of a man who laid new wooden floors in a home in which I once lived, installed French doors that opened onto a patio, and rebuilt part of the kitchen. He was a skilled craftsman who earned a good living as a member of America's middle class. Jesus was nothing like this.

It's quite mistaken to think of Jesus owning a business in which he built houses or made tables and chairs. This is a modern concept of a carpenter. Jesus belonged to a sector of society that was poor and powerless. Some scholars even believe he was from a class below that of peasant farmers and only one step above beggars.[13] If this is correct, his family owned no land, and he and Joseph scraped up whatever odd jobs they could to survive. For people at this impoverished level of existence, survival was everything.

Under Roman rule life was so harsh for the masses that there were frequent attempts at revolution, all of which were brutally crushed. Sometimes hundreds were crucified along the roadside. The repeated failure of these uprisings led to despair.

During the first century of our era, this despair gave rise to a number of movements that saw God as the only hope. If Israel were ever to be a free people, God would have to intervene.

John the Baptizer warned of an imminent judgment on the corrupt, unjust social system that oppressed people. He initiated his followers into what he believed would be the messianic age by baptizing them. But instead of building a community in the desert to await God's intervention, as other charismatic leaders had sometimes done, he sent everyone back to their homes. In this way he was seeding society with people who were prepared for the advent of the messiah.

Living on the edge economically all his life awakened Jesus to the realization that the average person had no opportunity to experience any kind of meaningful life. His awareness of the unfairness of society moved him to want to make a difference. At first he identified with John the Baptizer and was baptized by him, but soon he began his own movement. This movement was unlike any movement Palestine had ever seen. Its unique flavor flowed from Jesus' understanding of himself.

To be true to himself meant that Jesus had to take a tremendous risk. Already on the fringe economically, he had to abandon the only material comfort he knew and drop into the homeless class to pursue what his heart was leading him to do. His home became the homes of other people and the great outdoors. "Foxes have holes and birds of the air have nests," he said of this period of his life, "but the Son of Man has nowhere to lay his head."

THE PRICE OF BEING YOURSELF

One of Jesus' strangest statements points to how much courage it takes to be who you really are. He said, "I have come to 'set a man against his father, a daughter against her mother, and a daughter-in-law against her mother-in-law'; and 'a man's enemies will be those of his own household.'" This doesn't sound like the Jesus who taught us to love each other. Why would Jesus want to set family members against one another?

He explained, "If anyone comes to Me and does not hate his father and mother, wife and children, brothers and sisters, yes, and his own life also, he cannot be My disciple." Jesus wasn't advocating hatred. He was describing a stage people had to pass through if they were to enter the promised land of their inner being.

Western culture emphasizes independence, being your own person, and standing on your own two feet. We prize freedom and individuality. But these are modern values that didn't exist in the world in which Jesus grew up. To understand Jesus' words, we must realize that in first-century Mediterranean culture, family life stifled individuality. The idea of people being themselves was alien to first-century folk.

In those days, your individual identity was unimportant. What mattered was your social identity, drawn from the group you belonged to. The primary group was the family, and beyond that the village, tribe, and nation.

Your first responsibility was to fulfill the expectations of your family. In that world, family owned you, and you owed them your allegiance.[14] The idea that you might want to do something of your own was unacceptable. You married the person chosen by your family, were told where to live, and had your life's work cut out for you. The father of the family was the authority, with the right to command and to punish. He determined your role in the family, and your role is what gave you your sense of who you were. You knew your place in life, and your place defined you.

Our values are different. If someone asks us to marry them, most of us aren't interested in whether such a marriage would unite two farms, bringing greater honor to the family. We want to know that our suitor loves us. But back then, an individual's desires, feelings, and preferences didn't come into the picture. What was good for the family, tribe, or nation was all that mattered. Indeed, to defer to family was understood to be the will of God. The idea that God's will might lead you to go against the group was unthinkable.

When Jesus came onto the scene teaching the worth of the individual and urging people to listen to God within themselves, it was scandalous.

JESUS SHATTERED NORMAL VALUES

How revolutionary Jesus' message was can be seen from a story he told about a man who gave a great banquet and invited many guests. When the time for the banquet arrived, one said he had bought a field and needed to check it out. Another said he had bought five yoke of oxen and needed to test them. Yet another said he had recently married and needed to stay home.

The host expected the guests he had invited to the banquet to put his invitation ahead of their other obligations. When they sent excuses for not attending, he dispatched his servants to find people of every walk of life to replace them. To the amazement of everyone, the homeless beggars, the lame, and the blind were invited. At that time, such folk were considered cursed by God and treated as outcasts.

Surprisingly, Jesus' parable showed these most unfortunate of human beings to be in an advantageous position. Because they were alienated from society, they were free of obligations and therefore able to attend the banquet. This is why Jesus said, in a more literal translation of a statement in the Sermon on the Mount, "Blessed are you who are beggars."

Jesus' parable shocked society's sensibilities by reversing what, in those days, was considered honorable behavior. It challenged people to behave in a manner that was deemed dishonorable!

That Jesus' parable reversed customary politeness isn't immediately apparent to readers in our time. We assume the reasons people didn't go to the banquet were lame excuses. For us honorable behavior would mean canceling only in an emergency.

But what was honorable behavior in that society? The family farm, the family oxen, and spending time with a new wife took priority. So important was family that even if there were a war, a young man was excused from the military for the first year of his marriage.

Jesus' parable shattered these values. It asked people to attend the banquet ahead of family, something unheard of in that society.

Echoing this parable, Matthew's version of the Lord's Prayer says, "Forgive us our debts as we forgive our debtors." Becoming part of the kingdom of God releases a person from an identity defined in terms of fulfilling one's obligations to society.

"You owe it to us," said family.

"No, that debt's been canceled," said Jesus. "God's will for your life takes precedence. You owe it to God to be true to yourself."

HOW DO YOU TAKE UP YOUR CROSS?

When Jesus left home at around age thirty and became the leader of a movement, his mother, brothers, and sisters became concerned about him. Word reached them that people were saying, "He's gone mad!"

Thinking they had a right to order him home for rest and recuperation, Jesus' family set out to find him. Arriving at a packed house in Capernaum where he was teaching, they attempted to get him to conform to their wishes as his family. Jesus responded, "Who are My mother and My brothers?" Pointing to his followers, he said, "Here are My mother and My brothers! For whoever does the will of My Father in heaven"—whoever becomes what the divine essence desires them to be, not what family expects them to be—"is My brother and sister and mother."

Jesus was strong enough to be close to people and still be completely true to himself. He didn't give up any part of himself to please others, and he had no need to be a rebel. He was simply himself, without apology. Though his family couldn't understand his determination to follow his own path, he remained loving to them. In time his unwavering love paid off. His mother was at his crucifixion, and after his death his brother James became the leader of the community he founded.

If Jesus' family wasn't initially supportive of him, the people of his hometown of Nazareth were ready to kill him. On a visit home, he addressed the congregation in the synagogue. Luke reports, "So all those in the synagogue, when they heard these things, were filled with wrath, and rose up and thrust Him out of the city; and they led Him to the brow of the hill on which their city was built, that they might throw Him down over the cliff."

To dare to be yourself in Jesus' world meant going against enormous pressure to conform. In a world that believed God to be a supreme being quite separate from and exalted above humanity, to claim that your true self was an aspect of the divine presence, and you therefore needed to listen to your inner voice, was unthinkable. Only people who had grown to hate society's stifling control of their lives mustered the courage to break free.

Because Jesus violated the conventions that governed everyone's lives, eventually not only his town but also his nation rejected him. Though he was no rebel but simply true to himself, he was handed over to the Romans for crucifixion, the punishment for fomenting rebellion.

To "take up your cross" is to pay the price of being true to yourself, a price that's different for all of us according to our various walks of life. This price is something you pay willingly for the chance to accomplish what you really want to do. For most of us it doesn't lead to a literal death. For an artist it may mean financial sacrifice. For a nurse, long and sometimes inconvenient hours. For a mother it may mean feeding her child before herself.

BEYOND INDIVIDUALISM

Many who followed Jesus in daring to be themselves were rejected by their families. Frequently they had to leave all they owned and everyone they loved. As Peter said to Jesus, "See, we have left all and followed you."

While many of us are only able to sustain a sense of ourselves by limiting our connection with others, Jesus' disciples learned from him that a rich network of relationships enabled them to express who they were more completely. After his death, the community that had formed around him became bound so closely that its members regarded themselves as brothers and sisters with responsibility for each other's welfare.

What united this community was divine love, welling up within each of them and flowing back and forth between them. People drew close to each other because in community they could more easily learn how to be the loving individuals they had *always* been in their essence.

The community that grew out of Jesus' teachings became an alternative family upon which responsibility fell for feeding, housing, and clothing those who had lost everything by bucking the status quo. This explains why, after Jesus' death, according to the book of Acts, those who owned fields or houses would sell them, bring the money received from the sale, and turn it over to the apostles to be distributed to each according to their need. Because people thought of themselves as brothers and sisters in the family of God, "neither did anyone say that any of the things he possessed was his own, but they had all things in common."

Jesus invites us to free ourselves from the limitations imposed upon us by family and society. He also calls us beyond society's notions of rugged individualism. In place of both of these restrictive lifestyles, he invites us into God's universal family. In this family, which he called the kingdom of God, people love each other for who they truly are, not only if they conform.

In Jesus' words, only by losing your life do you find it. To truly be yourself requires surrender of the image you have of yourself. You "deny" yourself as you've known yourself, resulting in nothing less than the "death" of your limited mental concept of yourself. When you take this courageous step, you become truly free. Life suddenly seems full of possibilities!

14

"YOU'RE ON YOUR OWN, YOU KNOW!"

—

To experience your divine nature in your everyday life requires you to *believe in yourself without apology*. This is something we all have enormous difficulty doing.

Why is it so difficult to believe in yourself?

Simply because you feel *guilty* whenever you risk being yourself. You're so used to apologizing for yourself, you daren't be yourself with nothing held back.

On the surface, guilt appears to come from doing wrong. But this is far too shallow an understanding of guilt. You can see it's too shallow when you think about how people often feel guilty even when what they are doing isn't wrong but simply in conflict with someone else's expectations.

What does it take to become an individual? You have to stake your claim in the world. "Mine!" is one of the early declarations a child makes as it plays with toys among other children.

But what happens when you begin to assert your rights as an individual and claim the freedom to be yourself?

"What on earth are you doing?" a parent demands of you. You have been caught deciding something for yourself, and what arises is a sensation of being "caught out." This feeling of being caught out is the feeling we know as guilt. Guilt goes hand-in-hand with the freedom to choose your own life instead of being what someone else wants you to be.

HOW WE LEARN TO FEEL GUILTY

How guilt is rooted in freedom can be seen in the case of a woman who all her life had been driven by her mother to achieve. At age two she entered her first beauty pageant. By three she knew her alphabet and was reading simple sentences. At four she was learning both piano and violin. Ballet and drama classes followed. Always a winner in her local town's pageants, her mother drilled into the girl that she was born to go places. "You'll be a movie or TV star someday," she assured her, pushing her to enter more and more contests. Believing fame to be her destiny, the girl complied.

In school this girl behaved like a little adult, was the favorite of all her teachers, and excelled in every class. She played in the school orchestra, was on the debating team, and became a cheerleader—"the one thing I really enjoyed," she recollects. When she graduated from high school, she was named valedictorian.

But at college, without her mother's enthusiasm to keep her going, the young woman's interest in the life that had been etched out for her flagged. When, in her second year, a girlfriend decided to become a flight attendant, she sensed that she too would enjoy the freedom of flying. But because she felt guilty for even thinking of disappointing her mother, she struggled on in school for a third year.

The young woman's guilt was linked with the growth of her self-awareness. Guilt accuses us when we even dare to imagine pulling away from our parents and breaking out into a life of our own choosing.

When this young woman finally quit school at the end of her third year, she didn't immediately tell her mother. She felt so guilty that only when she had enrolled in flight attendant school did she write with the news.

When the mother learned her daughter had chosen to be a flight attendant, she responded, "Well, it's your life. But how you can enjoy passing out plastic cups in a jammed cabin is beyond me." What the mother was really saying was, "How dare you become aware of yourself as an individual, with a right to claim a life of your own?"

Guilt arises when you break with the traditional behavior of an ordered group that encloses you, such as your family, a club you belong to, or your church. When you meet with disapproval, you likely either comply and shut down, or you become a rebel, telling yourself, "Heck, I'm going ahead anyway!" You go about your own business, even though all the while, in the background, you don't feel good about what you are doing.

SELF-CONSCIOUSNESS PRODUCES GUILT

We are faced with a terrible choice. Either we insist on being ourselves and set ourselves up for rejection. Or, afraid of the repercussions, we hold back from doing what we really want to do and consequently fail to let our natural gifts flower.

Simply by being yourself, you feel unacceptable. Just by wanting to make your mark on the world, you become alienated. A failure to recognize this as the source of guilt is why so many Christians feel guilty so much of the time. Just to *exist* often makes us feel guilty!

It's this dilemma of how you can be yourself and also connect with others that Jesus addressed when he said, as the Greek might literally be translated, "The kingdom of God is *within and among you.*"

EVIL ARISES FROM GUILT

The divine within you thrusts you toward independence, but you feel badly for wanting to be independent. If you become warped by this guilt, you may attempt to corner a part of reality for yourself in ways that injure other people. This is how evil arises.

We engage in terrible acts not because we are prone to evil, but because to be our true selves hasn't been acceptable. Feeling outlawed for wanting to stake our claim on life, a voice somewhere inside whispers, "Well, you're on your own anyway. If you don't look out for yourself, who will?"

Since we already feel bad for wanting to look out for ourselves, it becomes easier to tell ourselves, "I'm in trouble anyway, so I may as well go all the way." This is how great evil begins in little ways. Because the real source of evil is our alienation from ourselves, once alienated, we can justify even the most selfish acts.

How was Jesus able to escape the guilt that's our universal condition?

As Jesus grew in his awareness of his oneness with God, he experienced a certainty that he was totally accepted. It was this sense of being accepted by God that drove his detractors crazy. How dare he believe he had God's approval?

Jesus' ability to be himself without feeling guilty made people conscious of the guilt that ran through their entire makeup. Face-to-face with him, they were confronted with how they had restricted their lives because they couldn't stand the guilt that would arise if they dared be true to themselves. He also made them angry because he awakened the regret they experienced for the limited individuality they *had* settled for.

In our own time, I heard tell of a Jewish man who chose to marry a Muslim. His father disinherited him. "You are a traitor not only to your family," he told his son, "but to the faith of all your ancestors! If you go ahead with this marriage, the family will regard you as dead!"

Why would this father cut his son out of his life rather than accept a Muslim bride into the family? When the father was twenty, he had fallen in love with a Catholic woman. Forbidden to marry outside the faith, he had instead entered into a marriage that for more than thirty years had been loveless. To support his son's choice of a wife meant opening up the pain of his own decision to conform to his family's wishes instead of acting in freedom. This was a pain he simply couldn't face.

Those who risked proximity to Jesus had their whole guilty existence exposed. This was an enormous threat. Some couldn't tolerate it and later either deserted him or condemned him.

But those who managed to tolerate the pain of this exposure experienced a piece-by-piece dismantling of their guilty worlds—a prerequisite for the flowering of the Christ reality in all our lives, which involves being true to ourselves.

15

FREE YOURSELF FROM YOUR GIANT "NO!"

—

"Repent and believe the good news," Jesus invited.[15] To repent means to change how you feel about yourself, and it results in "remission of sins." It enables you to let go of the guilt you've been carrying and at last feel good about yourself. You experience *self-forgiveness*.

People have generally thought of forgiveness in terms of being forgiven for particular transgressions. But with Jesus forgiveness had a far greater sweep. The forgiveness he extended to people penetrated much deeper than the specific wrongs they committed. It cut to the core of all offenses, to the *reason* people do the things they do. It went to work on the fact they didn't feel good about themselves. This is where his forgiveness was so much more radical than the forgiveness offered by traditional religion.

Hearing that Jesus was speaking to a crowd that had gathered in a house in their town, a paralyzed man's friends carried him to the house. When they couldn't get near Jesus because of the crowd, they removed a part of the roof and lowered the man down into the house on a mat. Seeing their faith, Jesus said, "Man, your sins are forgiven you."

The imagery of paralysis illustrates how our failure to believe in ourselves, and hence our resistance to growing into a more and more wonderful person, restricts our freedom to enjoy life. Jesus not only brought healing to this man's crippled body, but more importantly brought liberation to his whole being. From his motionless state, the man was freed to stand on his own two feet, walk, and run. He could be himself at last, enjoying a full life.

The religious leaders who witnessed this event were offended by Jesus' pronouncement that the man was forgiven. None but God can forgive, they objected. To which Jesus responded, "Which is easier, to say, 'Your sins are forgiven you,' or to say, 'Rise up and walk?'"

The brilliance of Jesus was to link forgiveness with the freedom to stand up and walk. Forgiveness is a change in how you feel about yourself that frees you from your limitations. Experiencing forgiveness and feeling fantastic about yourself are one and the same.

TO REPENT IS TO SEE YOURSELF DIFFERENTLY

"Repent," said Jesus. Few words have been more distorted in meaning in two thousand years of the Christian tradition than this word.

To repent has typically meant to feel sorry for being the person you are. But repentance isn't rejection of yourself, it's embracing yourself. *It's being sorry for not being yourself.*

Repentance isn't saying, "Look at all the bad things I've done. I must be a terrible person." Repentance isn't just to regret the past, it's to let go of the past and go beyond it.

Repentance means learning to hate "sin." Since sin springs from self-doubt, to hate sin means you reject the insecure way you've come to feel about yourself. When you repent, you no longer indulge in self-doubt.

Each of us has learned to assess ourselves through the eyes of others. At the age when this habit was formed, we had no alternative. Our full consciousness hadn't yet developed, which meant we were incapable of thinking rationally about the events that happened to us, and hence couldn't put them in perspective.

In repentance, you go easy on yourself for the things you've done. You forgive yourself, knowing that at the time you could do no better. You say, "How could I possibly have behaved any differently, seeing how little I knew my real self?"

How do you change the way you feel about yourself?

It's not just a question of telling yourself positive things about yourself. To change how you feel about yourself, you have to allow the pain of your formative years to surface so that you can address this pain with your adult mind. The pain is surfacing anyway, every day of your life, in your behavior and moods. But it's not being addressed in a manner that can heal it. Repentance addresses the pain in a way that ends it.

When I speak of addressing your pain, I'm not talking about simply rehashing the ways in which you were wounded. That isn't helpful. It only keeps you stuck. I'm talking about allowing the pain to become conscious, which will allow it to be dissolved by the powerful presence of your divine essence.

For example, self-hatred often manifests as awkwardness. To dissolve self-hatred means not giving into the awkwardness. Instead, you observe how awkward you feel, and you go forward anyway.

I'm not talking about doing things you truly don't want to do—things that simply aren't you. These are a matter of choice. I'm talking about feeling awkward in situations you wish you could enjoy but can't. We all know the difference between not caring to do something, and wanting to do it but feeling awkward.

If you keep the awkwardness conscious—"This is just awkwardness, not the loving person I really am"—and don't allow it to go underground so that you act it out by avoiding situations in which you feel awkward, it melts into self-acceptance.

God doesn't intend you to spend your life in recovery. God wants you to "sin no more." Repentance brings about a complete recovery. You recognize how your pain has unconsciously controlled you by causing you to feel less than the wonderful person you are.

Instead of being nervous about your contribution to life, telling yourself you lack competence, repentance requires you to identify this as only a voice in your head. Once you recognize it's just what you learned to think about yourself when growing up, you can focus on what you have to offer. You don't settle for mediocrity, doing without the fullness of life. You don't settle for isolation, feeling inadequate whenever you get into relationships. By not settling, your giant "no" to life becomes a powerful "yes." You begin to believe the good news.

FAITH IS FEELING GOOD ABOUT YOURSELF

To believe the good news means reclaiming a sense of yourself as good. Jesus was inviting you to dare to believe in and live from your true self. This is the divine Self within you, which is good. Repentance makes belief in yourself possible.

When we know we've been at fault, you and I cringe when we hear how fundamentally good we are—and therefore how good we are capable of being.

This essential goodness of the individual is what Jesus showed to those whose lives he touched. Whereas the religious institutions of the day rubbed people's noses in their failures, Jesus inspired in them a sense of their greatness.

Because God isn't separate from you but is your essence, to believe in God is to accept yourself. It's to stop feeling bad for exercising your freedom as an individual, distinct within the group. It's to cease being apologetic for yourself.

The trouble is, we don't like to give up apologizing for ourselves. We're comfortable with the discomfort of feeling apologetic because this is the only way we can ever remember feeling. It doesn't feel safe to feel good because such a feeling is so unfamiliar. There is a certain security in identifying ourselves as among the sick, the wounded. To see ourselves as a "victim" at least gives us an identity!

To believe the good news is to cease thinking of yourself as unsatisfactory. Instead of indulging in your usual tortured self-talk, you quiet your thoughts. You don't concentrate on all the things you think are wrong with you, or all the terrible things you've done. Rather, you allow the good feeling at your center to replace your self-recrimination. As this good feeling surfaces in you, it spontaneously changes how you feel about yourself. It eclipses the way you've learned to see yourself. You experience the falling-away of layer upon layer of disbelief in yourself.

As your true self revels in the freedom to *be* and to *enjoy*, you forgive yourself for limiting your love of yourself and of life!

JESUS FREES US TO BE OURSELVES

In the common interpretation of Christianity, God forgives our sins because of the crucifixion of Jesus. This forgiveness is intended to inspire in us a resolution to change.

But in this interpretation, forgiveness doesn't bring about the end of sin. The battle with sin remains a lifelong struggle. You believe you can never really change, never truly become free. You continue to think of yourself as a sinner.

This is a massive distortion of what Jesus taught. "If the Son makes you free," he insisted, "you shall be *free indeed*."

When Jesus told people to "sin no more," he wasn't simply issuing a stern warning, intended to dissuade them from sin. He was awakening in them an awareness that it *really was possible* for them to "sin no more."

Perhaps you hear "go and sin no more" as a judgmental voice: "Don't dare mess up again!" Jesus meant it as the liberating voice of your potential: "Go and be who you really are!"

The kind of forgiveness Jesus introduced into people's lives wasn't a cosmetic covering up of past destructive behavior. It tackled all harmful behavior at its root, solving the problem forever. Says the first New Testament letter of John, "Whoever is born of God does not sin." Forgiveness empowers us to "sin no more" because we enter into an entirely different understanding of ourselves that no longer permits us to stay stuck in destructive patterns.

If you continue to be trapped in unhealthy lifestyles, it's because you don't yet truly recognize your real self as mirrored in Jesus. As John explains, "Whoever sins has neither seen Him nor known Him." When you *really* see who you are, then you begin to live the kind of life Jesus lived.

John speaks of "abiding" in Jesus as the key to becoming free of self-destructiveness. To "abide" is to be able to maintain your understanding of yourself as part of the Christ. "Whoever abides in Him does not sin," John insists. In fact, anyone who has come to know themselves by meeting their true self in Jesus "cannot sin." To be free of sin doesn't mean you don't make mistakes or that you are perfect. It means you are no longer stuck in old patterns. In other words, once you have a solid sense of who you are, you are forever changed.

Jesus knew that only through repentance and forgiveness—changing your thoughts and feelings about yourself—can your real self emerge. As you learn to master yourself, not allowing the way you've seen yourself ever since childhood to dominate you, the shackles of limitation are loosed.

16

THE MOST BEAUTIFUL THING YOU CAN EVER EXPERIENCE

—

Jesus' effect on the common people of his time was electric. They flocked to be with him and loved his company. What was the source of his magnetism? What was it about him that they found so immensely attractive?

Jesus was the opposite of what people usually thought of as a holy person.

To the people of Jesus' day, to be holy meant to be God-fearing, subdued, restrained. The most holy of lives was a restricted life in which people gave up pleasure. John the Baptizer epitomized what people thought of as a holy man. He avoided gourmet foods, alcoholic beverages, and social activities such as parties and dancing.

John and Jesus are portrayed as opposites in the gospels. John the Baptizer "came neither eating bread nor drinking wine," said Jesus. Of course, Jesus wasn't suggesting that John declined food and water. He was referring to John's avoidance of feasting and the consumption of alcoholic beverages. In contrast, Jesus enjoyed both "eating and drinking." People derided him as "a friend of tax collectors and sinners!" Not only did he like to eat and drink, but he did it in the company of people whom society considered outcasts—people who loved to party.

Indeed, Jesus' exuberance for life was a scandal in his day. Feasting and drinking with the common folk were so much a part of his routine that the pious said of him, "Look, a glutton and a drunkard." The gospels show us a Jesus who feasted when food was on the table and who danced when the pipes played.

JESUS WANTS YOU TO ENJOY YOURSELF

For a reason they didn't understand, the pious found the exuberance of Jesus offensive. They couldn't equate the thoroughly human Jesus, who seemed to enjoy life like no one they knew, with their notions of what it was to be holy.

Jesus could "live and let live." He was far too liberated, too convivial, too ready to have fun for their liking. In fact, he was just the opposite of what they thought of as God-fearing. His was not a typically religious life, for there was nothing "saintly" or "holier than thou" about him.

Jesus' continual experience of joy mirrored a rapture that the religious had lost touch with in their upbringing. To be around Jesus made them terribly defensive, so much so that they felt they had to eliminate him. They couldn't tolerate him because he reminded them of what they had lost, yet yearned for.

While the religious community thought of Jesus as a "sinner," those who were closest to Jesus and knew him intimately described his authenticity as being "without sin." They didn't mean that Jesus never made mistakes from which he learned. They meant that he lived life from the heart with every fiber of his being. He embodied wholeness. This was what the religious people of his day didn't know how to do.

In Jesus, people encountered someone who was more real than anyone they had ever known. He exuded a love of life and a love of people that flowed from the core of his being.

While the religious frowned on having a good time, those close to Jesus felt him coaxing them into an enlarged life. He invited them to enjoy life "abundantly"—to live in a manner free of the restrictions endorsed by the religion of the day.

Jesus liberated people so that they too could begin to live exuberantly.

WHY PEOPLE SETTLE FOR MEDIOCRITY

All of us find a way to be more or less comfortable, despite our discomfort with ourselves.

This state of equilibrium is a compromise between ourselves and the world in which we grew up. We learn to think of ourselves a certain way. Our tastes, interests, preferences in friends, and sense of our gender form a picture of who we are.

This compromise is a decision against life. Ironically, by settling for being "comfortable," we are choosing a condition that isn't at all comfortable.

Consequently, when we are offered the possibility of experiencing ecstasy, we are terribly indecisive. We want to be happy, but we resist changes that could lead to happiness. In fact, we protect our mediocrity passionately!

This is why many of us become such *killjoys*. We are afraid to feel too much pleasure, and we don't want anyone enjoying themselves overly much around us lest they touch the nerve of our lost joy. God forbid that anyone should party like Jesus!

Do you see why Jesus, who epitomized joy, was crucified? The pious, who are the most shut down of all, couldn't stand the light he shone on their deadness.

To protect ourselves from feeling the awful pain of the loss of our original ecstasy, we create religions that *forbid* us to enjoy life too much. We enshrine our fear of disappointment in taboos that suppress any desire for such bliss. Whenever we are about to have fun, we imagine a God with a stern look uttering, "Thou shalt not!"

When it comes to our sexuality, many of us have an especially difficult time celebrating who we are. This is because to enjoy sex means claiming a part of reality for our own enjoyment in a way that affects another in the most personal of ways. Little wonder that sex tends to have so much guilt attached to it! It's the most dramatic example of the universal life-force being used in a private way.

In sex, you are cornering off someone, claiming them for yourself. In a very real sense, you are "using" someone else for your own pleasure, and they are using you. Using the universal life-force in a manner that is so highly personal makes us extremely self-conscious. It triggers all kinds of guilt. Are we really supposed to enjoy each other *this much*?

The most beautiful reality any of us can ever experience is our own self in communion with another. Love is an experience of knowing your true self in the presence of another. You are more fully yourself in the act of loving than at any other time. Love is a celebration of who you are.

People read that we are meant to be "crucified with Christ" and immediately think it's talking about self-denial. We must suppress our bodily urges, they conclude. Jesus is perceived as being against having a good time, and Christianity has been largely a religion of self-denial.

In what sense are we to be "crucified with Christ?" Our true self can come alive only to the degree that our false self, which resists the fullness of life, is put to death. We must die to all that robs us of an abundant life.[16]

To see the cross as a symbol of contempt for our humanity is a perversion of Jesus' death. The cross represents our refusal to embrace our humanity. Jesus, who embraced his humanity, died at the hands of those who refused to embrace theirs.

The self-fulfilling life, embraced with passion, has been terribly stigmatized. But in reality such a life is the most beautiful thing in the cosmos. When you are comfortable with yourself, you confidently stake your claim on life. Indeed, you *enjoy* doing so.

BREAKING FREE

Breaking out of mediocrity doesn't come easily. It requires facing up to why you settle for a mundane existence. Why do you cling so tenaciously to your mediocrity? Why, when you are equally capable of it, do you resist the rapture Jesus knew?

The inability to embrace life is no mere weakness. There runs through humans a *resistance* to an ever-greater fullness of life. This resistance is the very essence of sin. It's a refusal to be the glorious individual you already are.

Jesus didn't resist his greatness. Desire for life's fullness drew him along an unfaltering trajectory of growth. He wasn't held back by the huge inertial force that operates below the level of our conscious decisions. This is why he is described as sinless.

Little children are the natural subjects of the kingdom of God, Jesus said. The enthusiasm of a young child who hasn't yet learned to deaden such excitement was characteristic of Jesus' whole being. He was sinless because he allowed this good sense of himself to expand, as he learned to live ever more fully.

Filled with a sense of his goodness, Jesus was free of the contradiction of wanting to feel blissful yet being afraid to be so. His every day was an expression of overflowing joy, infinite peace, and a deep love of life. As his life touched the lives of his disciples, he awakened their long-forgotten sense that to exist should be an ecstatic experience.

To make this discovery is what it means to be a disciple of Jesus. How Jesus leads us into the freedom to be ourselves without reservation is what his crucifixion is all about.

17

WHY DID JESUS
HAVE TO DIE?

—

In the troubled times in which Jesus lived, talk of the messiah and anticipation of an end to Roman rule were rife. Speculation about the identity of the messiah abounded.

Jesus was the most charismatic of a slew of contenders. His fame had spread from Galilee to Judea. His meteoric rise had been noted in Herod's palace and hadn't escaped the attention of Pilate, the Roman consul.

Jews from far and wide were flocking to Jerusalem for the annual celebration of Passover. According to Jewish tradition, Passover commemorated Israel's release from Egyptian oppression a thousand years earlier. Would this Passover see the end of Roman oppression?

The people were in a state of high anticipation as word spread that Jesus was approaching the city and would be there in time for the festival. The disciples' spirits must have soared when, nearing the outskirts of the city, Jesus mounted a donkey, reenacting King Solomon's royal ride to his coronation ten centuries earlier, and crowds lined the road to cheer.

The disciples' hopes must have been high, too, when Jesus made several public appearances during the next few days. Everywhere he spoke, crowds pressed around him. The temple authorities, disturbed by the enormity of his popularity and fearing a Roman backlash, met to consider how they could silence him. But he had broken no Roman law that would warrant his arrest.

Despite Jesus' evident acclaim, as the week progressed, an uneasiness spread among his followers. Not only did he make no move against the occupying Roman forces, he seemed bent on antagonizing the authorities of his own nation. When he ransacked the temple, it was such a scandalous act that it was as if he were trying to provoke opposition. There grew within the disciples an uncomfortable feeling that their leader was wedded to a path of self-destruction, and this horrified them.

On the eve of the Passover, as Jesus ate with the disciples, he spoke plainly about the events that were about to unfold. Paraphrasing his words, "You'll all wish you had never known me." Peter objected that he would never desert Jesus. His protest met with the blunt rebuff (again paraphrasing), "You? You'll be the worst of all. You'll deny you ever knew me!"

The disciples' heads must have spun as, less than a week after being acclaimed by the masses, the religious leaders arrested Jesus secretly and turned him over to the Romans on trumped-up charges. By the next morning Jesus hung like a common criminal on a Roman cross.

A SELF-CHOSEN DEATH

To many who had cheered as Jesus entered Jerusalem, he was just another in a long line of failed, would-be messiahs, his crucifixion a plan gone wrong.

To the disciples, Jesus' final days were utterly baffling. They could make no sense of his behavior. Jesus appeared to anticipate and welcome defeat, playing into the hands of those who wanted him dead. Even at his arrest, when Peter pulled a sword to protect him, he ordered that there be no resistance and that they allow him to be taken quietly.

The disciples likely thought back to a conversation at Caesarea Philippi on the way to Jerusalem. Jesus had tried to explain that things might not turn out in the glamorous way they imagined. When he suggested that going to Jerusalem would result in his execution, the disciples wouldn't hear of it. Peter protested, "Far be it from You, Lord;

this shall not happen to You!" Jesus rounded on Peter, telling him he didn't understand the messiah's mission.

It was clear now to the twelve that in journeying at the time of Passover to the seat of Jewish economic, religious, and political power, Jesus had deliberately invited execution, his timing precise.

But why would someone riding the crest of a mass movement choose to end such a stellar career in a death that, had he only asked his followers to take up their swords, may have been avoidable? Was Jesus a masochist?

Had Jesus intended to start a religion of suffering and invite others to imitate him by suffering also, he would certainly have been a masochist. But his Christ self took no delight in suffering.

The agony of Jesus' death wasn't meant to extol suffering, as if suffering were a virtue and could somehow appease an external God. Though he embraced his death, describing it as the very hour for which he had been born, *he rejected suffering as a way of life.*

That Jesus had no appetite for suffering, no desire to experience a Roman crucifixion, is evident from the hours immediately before his arrest. In the Garden of Gethsemane, he struggled with accepting the crucifixion that lay ahead. Was it truly his Christ self that was drawing him into this destiny? Faced with excruciating suffering, he had to be sure of himself.

"Not My will, but Yours, be done" was not a commitment to a victim's death, but to the culmination of his whole life's meaning. In those three hours of prayer in the garden, we see him coming to a full acceptance of crucifixion as the only way for him to be true to everything that made him the person he was. When he emerged from the garden, it was with a certainty that could only come from his divine essence.

JESUS INTENDED TO CHANGE THE WORLD

For Jesus to embrace his death makes sense when we realize that his life was dedicated to changing the world. His intention was to show us how to end our alienation from ourselves, and hence from each other. He died to demonstrate how human suffering can be eradicated.

Jesus recognized that to respond to those who sought his death with violence would not bring the peace and prosperity for which people long. Had he taken up the sword, he would have been remembered as just one more leader in a long history of bloody revolutions, none of which ever brought about the utopia of which their champions dreamed. Instead, he chose the one way that could finally end oppression and the suffering it causes—a revolution of the heart.

Society systematically suppresses the joyfulness with which we are all born. Underlying everything we do as a human race, from education to economics, piety to politics, is this denial of joy. To compensate for the vague sense of having lost something, people who don't have access to their ecstatic, divine center seek to live like gods on a material level—an illusion they achieve only by treating others as inferiors. Hence we live in a world of great inequality and suffering. Because Jesus knew all humans to be divine, he sought to awaken the joy in everyone. Then no one would need to pump up their ego at the expense of others. The world would be liberated from the tyranny of the roles of oppressor and oppressed.

Jesus' death was the unavoidable outcome of aligning himself with the ecstatic presence of God at the core of his being, in a world that crushes the divine ecstasy in people—and crushes all who attempt to awaken it in others. How dare he live a divinely ecstatic life in a sin-dulled world?

Jesus' unapologized-for ecstasy challenged the way the whole world works. This is why he said that his kingdom isn't of this world. It undermines the entire oppressive system in which humans function. It ushers in a completely *new* way of "doing a world," in which all are equal because all are offspring of God.

The route Jesus chose caused his disciples to think of him as "the savior of the world" in the sense that his death introduces all humans to the possibility of experiencing the fullness of their divinity. Thus Jesus ushers in the kingdom of heaven, in which everyone lives divinely, not just the few.

18

HOW YOU CAN ACCEPT YOURSELF

—

All of us want to be happy, yet few of us enjoy sustained happiness. Our experiences of ecstasy are usually fleeting, our rapture short-lived. Even if we try to keep our chin up, it takes effort. No sooner do we let our guard down than we lapse into feelings of inadequacy, negativity, and discouragement.

The feelings we experience aren't caused by our everyday dealings with people. They are in the background all the time, and events merely evoke them. Sadness and hurt surface as but the "tip of the iceberg" of our normal state. This is because beneath our best efforts, most of us are plagued by the feeling that we are a *victim of life in general.* We don't believe life is on our side.

Upbeat and outgoing though we try to be, the images we have of ourselves are laced with those of a victim. A part of us is *always* waiting for the other shoe to drop.

We might describe our background state as one of massive disappointment. This disappointment has formed the backdrop of our lives ever since we lost touch with our original bliss. Though we allow ourselves a measure of pleasure, we are afraid to feel too happy in case we are again disappointed. We would rather live in a state of discontent, peppered with upbeat moments, than hope to be happy continually and risk being plunged into painful disappointment again.

WALKING ON EGGSHELLS

Ecstasy is something for which all of us long wistfully yet resist when it's offered. In contrast, ecstasy was something to which Jesus' entire being uttered a resounding "Yes!"

For Jesus, feeling ecstatic was a continuous state. It didn't depend on things going well. Even in death, his ecstasy was undiminished.

We've seen that salvation means to be in a healthy state. It's to experience wholeness. The whole of you comes together in a grand symphony. In this state of being, there's no undertow of being a victim, which serves only to undermine enjoyment of life. Healed of your victim mentality, you accept yourself and embrace your life with the exuberance of Jesus.

Christianity has always proclaimed the saving power of the *blood* of Jesus. But how the blood of Jesus heals us of feeling like victims has been greatly misunderstood.

"Without the shedding of blood there is no remission" of sin, we're told. The usual interpretation of this is that God gave us freedom, which meant taking the risk that we might sin. When we disobeyed, the scales of justice were tipped against us. The penalty was death. The scales could only be balanced if someone who never disobeyed God were to die in place of us.

The idea that a bloody sacrifice is required before God can look upon us with favor springs from primitive belief in wrathful deities who, in the minds of their worshipers, demanded sacrifices upon pain of lightning bolts, drought and flood, earthquakes and tornadoes. The idea that God needs to be appeased with a bloody sacrifice is blasphemous.

To believe that God must be appeased is to remake God in the image of our own hurt and alienation. We imagine that God gets offended and lashes out like we do when people hurt us. God, as most people imagine God, is no better than an upset human. But such a God is nothing more than a projection of our human pettiness into the heavens.

We can never really experience peace as long as we believe that God must be kept happy. What kind of a peace would it be if, the moment we stepped out of line, we were in trouble? There could be no real

Sabbath rest, no true promised land. Life would be like a continual walking on eggshells.

The crucifixion shows us a God who is entirely different from a judge who threatens us with punishment or requires appeasement. Jesus on the cross introduces us to the merciful *nature* of God. He shows us *a God who forgives simply because it's God's way to forgive.*

Jesus' God is a God who liberates us from all threats—a God who is nothing but love. "There is no fear in love," says the first letter of John, "but perfect love casts out fear, because fear involves torment." God loves in a manner that generates no fear whatever.

GOD DOESN'T NEED TO BE APPEASED

The New Testament insists that God and humanity need to be reconciled for us to know peace. But it isn't God who needs to be reconciled to us, it's we who need reconciliation with our Christ self.

Atonement has to do with us, not God. We are the ones who have difficulty feeling accepted, loved, after we mess up. God has no problem with the fact we mess up, for God knows that we learn how to be our true selves by first finding out who we aren't.

It's often said that Jesus paid for our sins.[17] There is no such statement in the Bible. On the contrary, each of us pays for our own sins. "The wages of sin is death," says Paul, referring not to our natural death at the end of life but to the dead state humans live in when cut off from their essence. We live in ways that are killing us, reaping what we sow. As Ephesians puts it, we are "dead in trespasses and sins."

God doesn't need anyone to die, anyone to atone, anyone to become a sacrifice in order to forgive sin. No balancing of scales is necessary. The very idea is a projection onto God of a mistaken human sense of justice. The crucifixion has nothing to do with God forgiving sin. God has noble eyes and can only see his sons and daughters as perfectly lovable.

What does the crucifixion of Jesus have to do with us? Paul tells us that it depicts a death all of us suffer—the deadening of our Christ self by a world that doesn't recognize our divine essence. In the crucified Jesus, we see what we are really doing to ourselves when we don't embrace our identity as a daughter or son of God.

UNDERSTANDING JUDGMENT AND WRATH

As Jesus awakens us to our divine essence, we are spared from "wrath," as Paul wrote to the Romans. This happens as we come under divine judgment. God's wrath and God's judgment have been terribly misunderstood because so many images of God from prior to Jesus' unveiling of our divine nature have been projected onto these terms. Jesus brings us a correct understanding of God's wrath and God's judgment.

The wrath of God isn't something an external God inflicts on us. As Paul told the Romans, God allows us to experience "a debased mind." Completely unaware of our true self, we live entirely from an unenlightened state of mind, which results in us reaping the consequences of blundering our way through life. The "wrath" of God is the pain we inflict on ourselves—the self-hatred and unrest we feel within from living in ways that deny our divine essence.

The judgment of God is a healing process that ends our need to see ourselves as victims. This judgment will eventually extend to all humanity. Peter, in one of his letters, says that judgment begins "at the house of God." Those of us who are entering into the Christ experience are in the process of undergoing judgment. This judgment is experienced *internally*.

You begin to experience a tension between the life you are living and the deeper you that's seeking to emerge. As this tension grows, you find this deeper you "judging," or evaluating, your behavior. You are becoming conscious of your actions and their consequences, which triggers a desire to live responsibly.

As you recognize that you've been out of kilter with yourself, this eventually causes you to come to your senses.

GOD DIDN'T NEED A RANSOM—WE DID

Jesus died as a "ransom" for our sins. But God didn't need the ransom—we did. Jesus buys us back from the false way we've seen ourselves. He ransoms us by showing us that we don't have to live lives that fall short of who we really are. He claims for us our true divinity, reclaiming for us our potential.

Jesus died for *us*, not for God's benefit. He bore our sins on the cross, not so God could forgive us, but so that we could see, in the mirror of him crucified, what we have been doing to ourselves by not accepting a forgiveness that has always been ours.[18] There was no need to bring about any change in God's attitude to us because God has never been alienated from us.

The people of Jesus' nation didn't understand this, and consequently imagined themselves alienated from God whenever they did wrong. It was as if God had hidden from them, departed from them, separated from them because of their sins. At times they felt as if God had withdrawn the divine presence not only on an individual basis, but also from the nation as a whole. It was as if God's ears had become deaf to their cries.

These were very genuine feelings, experienced by those who wrote the psalms, as well as by the prophets. In the same way, many today feel as though the wrong they have done has caused God to withdraw from them.

But can you fall out with God? You can never fall out with God, except in the way you *think* of yourself in relationship to God. How can you, when God's presence extends everywhere? If you imagine yourself, or anyone else, as somehow separated from God, then you have a finite God. Being infinite, God *has* no "out." As the psalmist realized, if he descended into the depths of hell, even there he would experience God's presence. Of course! We will find God wherever we go because God is the heart of our own being. Only in our imagination can we be "outside" of God.

It's we who need leading back to awareness of God, not God to us. God's mercy has always been extended to us, even in our most messed-up state. "While we were *still sinners*, Christ died for us," says Paul. Indeed, he told the Corinthians that in the drama of the crucifixion, God was in Christ, reconciling *the entire world* to the divine Self instead of counting our failures against us.

For us to be reconciled to God requires that we stop projecting our bad tempers onto the God who is pure goodness and love.

We stop being afraid of God, because we recognize God as our own essence.

19

THE AGONY
AND THE
ECSTASY

—

When President John F. Kennedy said, "Ask not what your country can do for you, but what you can do for your country," it resonated with millions because the idea that we exist for others is a message we have heard all our lives. Childhood taught us that we are here not for ourselves but for our parents, and, in a broader sense, for society.

Each of us has been robbed of our *own* being and forced to *be for others*. As long as we are caught in this trap, we can never *truly* be for others.

What our parents could not face in themselves, they tended to take out on us. To the degree that they were damaged in childhood, they likely damaged us. The most basic form of damage is the denial of the right to be our own person. This is the greatest hurt we ever experience. Sexual abuse of a child is an extreme form of the way in which adults reduce children to a function of their own experience.

When we have been denied our essential individuality, we attempt to forget about the pain of this denial. Cut off from our potential for ecstasy, we content ourselves with the mediocre house we have had to build atop an emotional fault line. Our massive disappointment becomes buried in the decent existence of the good citizen, whose life is never quite fulfilling.

When we are not only denied our individuality but also abused, the abuse doesn't allow us to bury the loss of our individuality in the behavior of a good citizen. With the wound ever raw, we have little choice but to pass the abuse on, inflicting abuse on others. Our huge sense of disappointment can come out in the tyrannical behavior of a domineering mother or controlling husband. At the extreme, it can emerge as the sadism of the political monster, who directs his or her vengeance toward scapegoats.

JESUS BREAKS THE CYCLE OF ABUSE

The real tragedy of believing we are victims is that by doing this, we deprive ourselves of the awareness of our magnificent Christ self.[19]

The man on the cross represents simultaneously the person you have been forbidden to be, and the people that, as a result of being robbed of yourself, you have hurt.[20]

In the normal course of things, abuse is perpetuated from generation to generation. As the prophet Ezekiel put it, the fathers and mothers have eaten sour grapes, and the children's teeth have been set on edge.

Hurt, you tend to hurt others. Someone does you an injury, and you retaliate. Many Old Testament psalms express this desire for retaliation with amazing candor, demonstrating a level of honesty about our hostile feelings that we find unnerving. Victims can be vicious!

Through refusing to see himself as a victim, even under the circumstances of crucifixion, Jesus invites us to give up the dreary need to perpetuate our victim mentality.

BEYOND LIFE AS A VICTIM

Crucifixion points to the pain in which humans live each day. It's this pain that causes us to hurt both ourselves and each other. We can't talk ourselves out of this pain, and we can't talk others out of it. The crucifixion shows us to be people who cannot help but hurt both ourselves and others unless we come to know ourselves as fundamentally different from the deprived deprivers, the wounded wounders, the crucified crucifiers we have been.

Jesus, who was free of this pain, entered fully and willingly into our pain by allowing himself to be crucified by the pain of those who killed him. To wholly trumped-up charges and an unjust verdict, he offered no resistance. His acceptance of the trial and judgment he received at the hands of society touches a nerve in each of us.

On the hill of the skull, Jesus, the symbol of our true self, died, not feeling sorry for himself, but ecstatic. Ecstasy transcended agony. In his undimmed ecstasy, we see a reflection of our own inherent ecstasy, which has been buried beneath our feelings of disappointment and our image of ourselves as victims.

Jesus knew he was one with God. How can God be a victim? Once we embrace our Christ self, neither can we be victims. In Jesus' refusal to think of himself as in any sense a victim, we recognize that to see ourselves as victims is totally unnecessary.

This changes how we respond when we are hurt. There's a moment when we first feel wounded. At that instant, we believe ourselves to have been abused, but we haven't yet turned to blaming someone. This is the moment when we are at risk of buying into a victim mentality. It's at this moment that Jesus invites us to recognize our Christ self instead.

In other words, Jesus showed us that, no matter what has been done to us—no matter how victimized we think we have been—we don't have to be entombed in feeling sorry for ourselves, hitting out at others because of our pain, but can choose to remain peaceful.

YOUR REAL SELF IS INTACT

Our disappointment with life is healed when we embrace Jesus' "*Yes*" to the fullness of life. *He is a symbol of our innate capacity for joy.* It's by showing us this capacity as our basic state that he saves us.

Were Jesus a mere victim, a martyr like any other martyr, he would be of no help to us. Simply mirroring to us a victim mentality, sharing our misery with us, doesn't rescue us. It's no more life-transforming than the counselor who tells you, "I hear your pain." This does nothing to move you *beyond* your pain. It simply confirms it.

No mere martyr can transform our disappointment into joy. It's neither sympathy nor admiration that inspire change, but *being opened up to our true state, our original being in God.*

This is what Jesus shows us on the cross.[21] By allowing his ecstasy to come through no matter what was done to him, he opens us up to recognize that beneath all of our disappointment is a state of divine contentment.

Who you *really* are remains untouched by life's disappointments. Your Christ self knows nothing of being a victim.

20

ONLY YOU CAN CLAIM YOUR TRUE NATURE

—

We can never get from others the validation for which we yearn. If our divine greatness is to emerge, our sense of who we are must shift from a dependence on others to a reliance on our true self. This had to happen in Jesus' disciples. Their experience of becoming centered in their own essence is a model for how it can happen to us.

As Jesus and his disciples trudged the hills of Palestine together, they saw, through a variety of stressful situations, what it meant for Jesus to be himself. They watched him maintain his equilibrium when he was tired, dusty, and thirsty. They saw how he remained completely calm in storms at sea, while they feared for their lives. When crowds pressed upon him incessantly, demanding his time and attention, they observed him define his own agenda and set his own priorities. Threatened by the temple authorities, they watched him maintain an unflinching commitment to his mission, even when it meant certain death. Above all, they saw how he responded to his enemies not with venom but with love. In every dimension of his life, he exuded a total acceptance of himself and of others.

The disciples had been forced all their lives to be other than the individuals they really were, their authentic selves systematically squelched by society. But experiencing daily life with Jesus awakened in them a sense of themselves that was rooted in their Christ essence. In his presence, they were allowed to be themselves.

The disciples had admired Jesus, and he became their champion. When they were around him, they felt good and believed themselves capable of a greatness from which they had earlier shied away. But because the disciples' newly-discovered good feeling about themselves was a *reflected* sense of themselves, it worked only as long as Jesus was around. A borrowed sense of ourselves is always dependent on the person from whom we are borrowing it.

Jesus' intention was for the disciples' new sense of themselves to become permanent. For this to happen, it could no longer depend on him. It had to come from direct dependence on their own inner Christ self. This required a quantum leap in their understanding of themselves. How was this leap to be made?

The Gospel of John reports that on the eve of his arrest, Jesus told his disciples it was to their advantage that he leave them. If he didn't, the spirit could not come.

For the Christ spirit to be manifested in the disciples, he had to let them down. He knew it was the only way they could finally come into their own. They had to find their feet and stand tall, grounded in their *own* divine center, not relying on his support. As long as they had him to turn to, they didn't feel the necessity to enter into what he represented as a potential within them.

Throughout history people have invested their hopes in charismatic teachers and leaders. When their attempts to change things fizzle, their followers are bitterly disappointed. It was no different with the disciples.

Suddenly, Jesus was no longer around to inspire them. They had dedicated themselves to a man and his mission, abandoning their homes, careers, and families, only to be plunged into confusion as he willingly allowed himself to be arrested, tried, and executed.

As the arrest, trial, and crucifixion unfolded, the disciples realized that if they had let Jesus down by fleeing when he was arrested, as he predicted they would, *he had also let them down.*

The disciples now went through a crisis so intense that it seemed their lives had been shattered. They had believed in Jesus. They had sacrificed everything to follow him, putting their lives on the line.

How could he give up without even attempting to fight? How could he desert them?

A CRISIS CAN OPEN OUR EYES

That Jesus had let his followers down had begun to dawn on Peter even before the crucifixion. As this rugged fisherman watched the trial before the Jewish ruling council, shortly before Jesus was delivered to the Roman governor Pilate, he believed that Jesus was abandoning him—abandoning everyone who had dedicated themselves to his cause.

Feeling betrayed, the man who had been Jesus' star disciple became so angry, he now denied he even knew Jesus. Peter's denials shed light on the nature of the spiritual crisis into which the disciples were thrown.

Popular wisdom concludes that Peter betrayed Jesus because he was afraid. But had he been afraid, he would never have followed Jesus to the scene of the trial. Besides, he had shown himself fearless only hours earlier, at the arrest, by unsheathing his sword.

No, Peter's denial was caused not by fear but by bewilderment. He could make no sense of what was happening. He felt like Jesus had failed him. In his confusion, he became enraged, vehemently denying he even knew Jesus.

But as Peter observed the proceedings of the trial, what he saw in Jesus wasn't a weak-kneed individual who had backed down under pressure. He watched as Jesus' assailants shoved him, struck him, taunted him, and spat on him. Try as they may, they could draw no reaction from him. Neither could Peter detect in him any fear, nor the least trace of anxiety. Instead, Jesus manifested a serenity, a calmness, a centeredness that witnessed to a strength with which Peter was well acquainted—a resilience he had encountered in no other person.

When Jesus turned and looked him in the eye, Peter's anger evaporated. He knew that this was no coward who had cratered in the face of opposition. Here was the same man he had been drawn to along the shores of the Sea of Galilee, composed, fully in control of himself.

In that moment, Peter fell apart. Utterly bewildered by Jesus' actions, yet ashamed of ever doubting him, he fled into the night weeping bitterly.

Other leaders of movements inspired false hopes, and their movements collapsed when they died. But just as Jesus had intentionally led his followers from Galilee to Jerusalem and his crucifixion, unbeknown to them, even in his death he was still leading.

HOW A SENSE OF OUR TRUE SELF IS BORN

To the disciples, it felt as if they had been plunged into a living death. They were beyond all their coping skills.

In actuality, they were in loving hands. The kind of death they were experiencing was of their old sense of identity being taken over by their Christ nature.

In our deepest being, we intuitively know ourselves to be incarnations of the divine, though we have lost consciousness of God at our center to such a degree that we fight it. Consequently, we usually awaken only reluctantly, and often painfully, to what we have sensed about ourselves all along. Most of us do not come to *really* know ourselves as daughters and sons of the Creator except through crisis—the same painful crisis that the disciples experienced when Jesus abandoned them. Self-awareness usually must be forced on us.

Knowing the pain it takes for the Infinite to become a real presence in a person's life, Jesus engineered a situation that left the disciples with no way of escape. In the hours following the crucifixion, they hit bottom. With their dreams shattered, the disillusionment they experienced was overwhelming, their grief and despair unbearable.

There is no greater pain than the complete and total collapse of your defenses, triggering the loss of all hope and all sense of meaning. Few of us ever reach such depths. We pull the plug on our suffering, either finding a way to escape it or committing suicide, before we bottom out. We think we cannot tolerate such misery.

Permanent transformation rarely occurs unless you think you are about to go under. Only through such a "death" do you develop a fuller sense of yourself.

What seemed to the men and women who accompanied Jesus to Jerusalem to be a nightmare was in fact the work of the divine, inviting them to come alive. The painful crisis Jesus had precipitated in his disciples produced in them a radical transformation.

The virus of their divinity—the unconditional love Jesus had manifested—had entered the disciples' bloodstream forever. Try to kill it though they may, it had them in its grip. This is what Peter recognized when he broke down in tears.

On the other side of the crucifixion, captured in the image of the empty tomb, this sense of themselves as divine reasserted itself in the disciples with a power that claimed them. They were resurrected into fullness of being. They experienced within *themselves*, as themselves, the reality of God that Jesus experienced.

Everything Jesus had been to them now became *a direct experience of their true selves*, instead of a reflected sense of themselves that they borrowed from Jesus. The crisis they had experienced awakened them to see that *at the heart of each of us is the God for whom we search.*

21

JESUS' DEATH WAS THE BEGINNING OF THE END OF THE WORLD AS WE KNOW IT

—

For almost two thousand years the Western world has spoken of Jesus Christ as if "Christ" were his last name. But Jesus was never called this in his lifetime.

Christ, the Greek equivalent of the Hebrew term messiah, means "the anointed one." Anointing with oil was the traditional way in which Israel's kings were dedicated. As long as there was a monarchy, the Jewish people had a messiah—a christ. In the role of the christ, the king was the "savior" of the nation, a term that means deliverer. His task was to provide for the welfare of the people and deliver them from their enemies.

But in 587 BCE, Palestine was invaded by the Babylonians. The royal line dating back to King David came to an end. The nation no longer had a "christ," a messiah, on whom they could count for their well-being.

With the end of the monarchy, the people of Judea began to dream of the day when God would restore the throne. This wasn't a longing for the return of the monarchy as they had known it, because so many of their kings had failed to treat the people justly and hence were not true christs. Instead, the dream of a messiah came to embody the people's longing for an "ideal" king. This king would be like King David, a true savior of the people. He would free Israel from their enemies and usher in an era of peace, prosperity, and equality.

Jesus' followers thought of *him* as the hoped-for deliverer, the messiah or christ. Consequently they expected him to lead a political revolt.

To Jesus, the term messiah or christ implied something very different from the conquering king his followers imagined. We saw in Chapter 17 that, as "King of the Jews," Jesus was interested not in leading a violent revolution against the Romans, but in beginning a peaceful revolution in the hearts and minds of his followers—a revolution that would produce a loving community and ultimately a loving world.

Jesus embodied the love that will someday transform the whole world. He experienced a oneness with even his enemies, which enabled him not to react to them with hostility. As he went to the cross, he was completely centered. Because he was so composed, he was neither intimidated by nor reactive to the hatred heaped upon him. He responded to his tormentors with understanding, compassion, and love. His behavior sets the tone for the kingdom of God.

THE IMPACT OF JESUS' DEATH

To show how behaving in such a non-reactive manner can change the world, the gospel writers employ apocalyptic language. This is an imaginative form of writing that was popular among the Jewish people at the time. This kind of language wasn't to be taken literally, but symbolically.

The apocalyptic symbolism points to the *impact* of Jesus' death, which is ultimately worldwide. It's saying that this death, which seemed so insignificant to most people at the time, had global meaning. It portrays the sweeping nature of what Jesus accomplished when he modeled a loving response to his enemies, ending the "eye-for-an-eye" mentality that had dominated the world for so long.

In the gospels, while Jesus was on the cross, the sun is said to have been darkened for three hours. We're also told that "the earth quaked, and the rocks were split." This isn't a description of actual events at the time of Jesus' death. The language doesn't literally refer to a local eclipse and a local earth tremor at the time. Rather "the Earth" is shaken—the whole earth—and there is darkness over "all the land," which symbolizes the earthshaking collapse of the old world order.

In these apocalyptic descriptions of the effect of Jesus' death, the light of the sun goes out and the stars fall from the sky. In Matthew's Gospel, dead people rise from their graves. These images signify the end of the world as we have known it. They depict the complete collapse of the world order we are used to. What will emerge from this return to primordial chaos is a new creation, a completely different kind of world.

The gospel writers want us to see that Jesus' radically different behavior, when eventually practiced by everybody, will change the world beyond recognition. The new humanity he pioneers by loving his enemies will be so different from the world as we have known it, it will be as if the planet itself had been recreated. As Paul would later say, looking back on the crucifixion, at this moment all humanity died with Jesus. God made "all things new." From this moment on, a new world began coming into being. The second coming had begun and the kingdom of God had been inaugurated.[22]

A PLACE IN THE KINGDOM OF HEAVEN

"In my father's house are many mansions," Jesus said in the Gospel of John. "I go to prepare a place for you. And if I go and prepare a place for you, I will come again and receive you to Myself; that where I am, there you may be also."

At the mention of mansions, almost everyone thinks Jesus is describing the sweet bye and bye. Beverley Hills style mansions in heaven! But Jesus' words sound a lot less glamorous when you read a modern translation. "In my father's house are many rooms." Ouch! You only get a room, not a mansion?

In a sense, Jesus was talking about heaven, but not a heaven beyond the grave. It's a heaven that can be experienced now. It's the progressive appearance of the reign of heaven on earth.

Jesus spoke mainly to Jews, so he used terms they understood. What was "the father's house" to Jews? When Jesus strode into the temple, made a whip of cords, and drove out the sacrificial animals and the tradesmen who sold them, he ordered, "Take these things away! Do not make My Father's house a house of merchandise!" To a Jew, the father's house was the temple.

In the year 70 the temple was destroyed. The end of the temple as the father's house was signaled by Jesus in a conversation with a man called Nathaniel. "Hereafter you will see heaven open," he said, "and the angels of God ascending and descending *upon the Son of Man*." This refers to the story of Jacob, who, when he was traveling, became tired and used a stone for a headrest. You've heard of Jacob's ladder, but it's a poor translation. That night, Jacob dreamed of a giant "staircase" stretching between earth and sky, upon which the messengers of God go back and forth between the heavenly throne room and those to whom they are sent. When Jacob awakened, he was afraid and said, "This is none other than the house of God, and this is the gate of heaven!'" He then took the stone he had used as a pillow and set it up as a pillar stone to mark the spot. The place became known as Bethel, meaning "house of El"—house of God. Later the house of God was relocated in Jerusalem.

Jesus says that the father's house is no longer in any particular place but comprises all who become part of the new humanity of which he is the embodiment. In other words, you and I are the father's house. We are the community of the Son of Man, the new humanity that replaces the temple. We are God's abode. We are where Christ is because, in Paul's words, the Christ is being "formed in" us.

"I go to prepare a place for you," says Jesus. We have already seen how Ephesians says that God has raised us up with Christ and seated us with him in the *heavenly places*. We are right now blessed with "every spiritual blessing in the *heavenly places* in Christ." Note the present tense. We already have these blessings. Living the heavenly life is now.

What kind of "place" does Jesus prepare for us in the new humanity? The rooms attached to the temple, where the priests stayed when they were serving at the altar, symbolized service. Jesus is saying that all of us have a role to fulfill, a task to accomplish, a place to serve in bringing the new humanity to fruition.

A POTENTIAL IN ALL HUMANS

Jesus said that through his crucifixion, he would draw all humans to himself.

People have always sought champions to lead them—kings and queens, lords and ladies to reign over them. Many feel safe if someone is in charge. But to Jesus, all were royalty, all potential kings and queens of their own lives.

Instead of becoming another champion and exercising dominion over people, Jesus showed them that the messiah they were seeking already existed within them. He empowered them to become their own champions and to take charge of their destiny.

"At the *name* of Jesus every knee should bow," we are told. In the ancient world, people were named according to what they were. For every knee to bow at the name of Jesus is for each of us to recognize that Jesus' nature is the true nature of all of us. It is to acknowledge that we, like him, are "partakers of the *divine nature*."

WHAT IT MEANS TO SAY, "JESUS IS LORD"

If Jesus was thought of as the anointed king, he was also spoken of as "Lord." We are told that, in addition to acknowledging his name, "Every tongue should confess that Jesus Christ is Lord."

Says the book of Revelation, the kingdoms of our world are to become "the kingdoms of our Lord *and* of his Christ." The Lord is Jesus. We are his Christ. Our lives are about nothing less than the transformation of the whole world. We embody a new kind of humanity that will someday populate the entire earth.

The Roman Empire called its caesars "Lord." Ruling from Olympian heights, the caesar defined the nature of the empire. Jesus' disciples adopted this title for their leader. To the claim "Caesar is Lord," they responded, "Jesus is Lord."

In speaking of Jesus as Lord, we must purge our minds of all images of Jesus as raised to Olympian status. Jesus was a very different kind of lord from a Roman emperor. Instead of dominating, he empowered.

People want power because our world equates power with success. But Jesus smashes our images of what power and success are. In the Revelation, the exalted Jesus is described as "the lion of the tribe of Judah." But when the author turns to look at this lion, what he sees is a slain lamb. The contrasting images of the roaring lion and the slain lamb jar us, inviting us to understand anew what it means for Jesus to be "King of kings and Lord of lords."

It's not to the kings and lords of the present era that the Revelation refers when it says Jesus is King of kings and Lord of lords. The Revelation elsewhere explains that all who embrace their Christ self become kings. We reign in our own lives now, right here on earth, as Jesus did in his, not over other people at some future time. The kingdom of God is a community in which there is a leveling of status. It's a new kind of world in which service, not position, defines greatness. As Jesus said, if you want to be chief, be the greatest servant.

Jesus founded a community that was radically different from the world in which people seek to dominate each other. The movement that grew out of his life was composed of strong individuals who could truly be themselves and connect with each other at the deepest levels. But as those who knew Jesus died, the movement changed. It increasingly took on the features of the world around it.

As the community Jesus founded spread, those who were more removed from the direct impact of Jesus and his disciples found it increasingly difficult to accept what he had taught concerning the universal greatness of humanity. People's persistent sense of unworthiness generated a resistance to seeing themselves as part of the Christ. This led them to isolate Jesus from all other humans, elevating him to the level of a kind of superman.

Jesus was no longer seen as the reflection of our true selves. People began to think of him as a lord and king who, like the lords and kings of the nations, was above and beyond common humanity. His various titles, which originally linked him to the most authentic characteristics of our humanity, became ways of placing him above those he sought to elevate.

What was once Jesus' movement became a monolithic church structure that dominated people's lives as the old world order had done. Instead of uniting hearts, it divided and conquered. If you fell in line, you were included. If you thought differently, you were expunged.

Because of this, for many, Jesus in the role of king and lord came to look like the ultimate tyrant, prepared to destroy anyone who didn't align with him. For them, he was certainly not the loving expression of a God who is nothing but love.

Said Paul to the Corinthians, God is ultimately to become "all *in all*." God-consciousness, which is pure love, will ultimately permeate each and every life. This is what brings about "the salvation of the world," or in modern English, "the wholeness of the world."

As more and more of us discover the Christ nature within us, all that Jesus was is expressed in us. We truly become his body—his second coming—ending the hostility of the old world and flooding the "new creation" with love born of a recognition of our divinity and oneness with all.

22

CATCH THE CONTAGION OF COOPERATION

—

Someone does you an injury. You think to yourself, "This person has wronged me." You are upset.

You are also convinced that you are in the right and they are wrong, and you want to set them straight. In your head, you imagine an argument with the person, which of course you win because the other isn't there.

In such a situation, the person with whom you are in conflict holds a certain fascination for you. You experience a strange mixture of attraction and repulsion. Even though you feel the person is against you, you find yourself thinking about them. Despite all your attempts to pull away from them, you discover that you are emotionally glued together.

A useful image is the Chinese trick in which you put your fingers into a woven fingerstall. The more you try to pull them out, the tighter it gets. This is what happens in a conflict. The more you try to dominate your adversary in your thoughts, the more they attract you and the more you are caught.

You may try to forget what the person did, even try to forget the person. But they keep popping up in your head. You may say to yourself, "Why should that so-and-so bother me?" But the more you tell yourself not to be angry, the more angry you become—and then you become irritated with yourself for letting them get to you. The fingerstall tightens.

WE QUARREL WITH OUR MIRROR IMAGE

Jesus taught that, more often than not, the person you can't stand is exactly who you need in your life if you are ever truly to be yourself.

How does this work?

We speak of those who are very angry as being "beside themselves." In a quarrel, each person is in a sense "outside" themselves, no longer centered in themselves. Their minds are on each other as they tell themselves how impossible the other is.

This obsession with the other might be described as an "ecstasy of disliking." It's the polar opposite of the ecstasy that comes with being a loving person.

When Jesus said, "Love your enemies," he was showing us that bringing quarreling individuals together requires unilateral action. If there is to be resolution of the quarrel, someone must break the ice.

One of the parties must quit their obsession with the other, centering their attention back on themselves, their life, and the things they enjoy. They must become "at home" with themselves once again. Only when they are comfortable with themselves, and can present themselves to the other in a settled state of mind, can resolution occur.

This is what Jesus was talking about when he said, "Whoever slaps you on the right cheek, turn the other to him also." Was Jesus telling us to let people walk all over us? Not at all. What he meant by "slaps you on the right cheek" isn't an act of violence, but the ancient gesture of contemptuous dismissal in which the back of the hand, not the palm, is used. It's an insult, saying to the person, "You mean nothing to me!"

"Turning the other cheek" represents a surprise, creative response in which, by remaining connected with the person instead of pulling away, you say to them, "Look, here I am still, a person like yourself, despite your attempt to dismiss me."

By refusing to behave like a non-person, you demonstrate a comfortableness with yourself. By not reacting, not pulling away, you invite the person to reconnect with you.

WHAT QUARRELS ARE REALLY ABOUT

Quarrels reflect how we feel about *ourselves*. We lash out at others because of *self*-hatred, though this isn't easy to recognize.

It's not easy to see because, once the other picks up our attitude and starts reacting, they aid and abet us in our flight from ourselves. Caught up in a storm of reactivity to each other, we can't recognize that we are transferring our own self-hatred onto the other.

By reacting to us, the other is unwittingly cooperating in our game of saying that it's not ourselves that we hate, not ourselves that we fear, not ourselves with whom we are unhappy. As long as their response to us is reactive, we feel justified and can go on believing that our hatred has an object other than ourselves.

If the other stops reacting, they cut off the proof they have been affording us that they are the problem. We are thrown back on ourselves and forced to carry on inside ourselves the battle we were waging externally. Only now do we discover that we are off-center, not in control. In a sense, we are "out of our mind."

Uncomfortable with ourselves, we are uncomfortable with anyone who dares get close enough to us to touch our discomfort. This is the source of the anxiety, irritation, and rage that we experience toward others.

Jesus was free of self-hatred and therefore had no need to lash out. His love for his enemies spelled out a highly creative way of relating to people. His refusal to fight with them, coupled with his powerful sense of presence, stopped them in their tracks and constitutes a formula for changing the world.

COOPERATION IS CONTAGIOUS

When Paul said, "Even though we have known Christ according to the flesh, yet now we know Him thus no longer," he was emphasizing how we *do* know him within us and among us. Jesus creates a community in which "we" is the preferred pronoun. He shows each of us how to be "we" without losing "me." This empowers authentic connection based on genuine acceptance.

Someone who has reached inner peace will be a source of peace for others. Being at home with yourself is the key to resolving disputes, for it puts others at ease with themselves. Calming yourself down and centering yourself in your divine essence, you start being friendly. This invites friendliness. Indeed, unless you start being friendly, the quarrel won't end.

A quarrel mended draws two people closer together because, when people open up to each other, the relationship becomes more real. The self-disclosure involved causes us to see the other in a new light. Whereas before we may have seen only their external expression, they now take on the attractiveness of a *person*.

Mending a quarrel opens the door to friendship. Self-disclosure is the hallmark of friendship. While attraction can happen at first sight, there is no such thing as love at first sight, for love happens only when exposure of our deeper selves occurs.

When Jesus said to his disciples on the eve of his execution, "I call you friends," he proceeded to tell them what his intentions were and what, as a result, was about to happen to him. They argued with him, attempting to change his mind, but his course was set. Because they couldn't understand his actions, they even deserted him. But as they experienced him still loving them in the wake of their betrayal, the quarrel was mended and, after the resurrection, they grew to love him in a far deeper way than had been possible before his death.

Catching the contagion of cooperation is like discovering muscles you never knew you had. Two people get a sense of a different and much more satisfying way of relating to each other. They discover a cooperative as opposed to a competitive way of being together, which more and more people are coming to see as the only hope for the planet.

Realizing that cooperation is a better way of resolving disputes than fighting doesn't automatically alter our behavior, any more than discovering muscles automatically turns you into Superman. It takes practice for new behavior to become spontaneous. But the new behavior begins with the recognition that we don't have to become something different from who we are. Love *is* who we are in our essence. We simply haven't owned it.

23

TIES THAT BIND

—

When someone disappoints you or in some other way hurts you, often the pain you feel is out of all proportion to the offense. Why?

To be disappointed or hurt triggers acute awareness of the immense disappointment from childhood that normally remains in the background of our everyday lives. Because the disappointment we suffered was too painful to bear at the time, we repressed it. So we don't connect our present pain with its source. In fact, we resist making such a connection. We fear we'll discover an ill for which there's no remedy.

Since we don't know where all of this pain is coming from and therefore can't heal it, we try to defend ourselves against more pain by lashing out at anyone we perceive as hurting us.

When we have been hurt by someone, we tend to seek allies. It's usually not difficult to find someone who will agree that the person who offended us is an ass. This is especially so if the other person is actually in the wrong. If we can bolster our case by pointing to others who have been hurt too by this person, we feel all the more strongly that our sense of being a victim is justified.

Once we have a consensus that the other party is at fault, our preoccupation with this person intensifies. The person is now seen as the cause of angst in our life, the source of much dissatisfaction. The person has become a scapegoat.

Scapegoating is a way of managing the enormous pain of our disappointment with life, which is awakened whenever someone hurts us.

The world divides people into *us* and *them*. "They" then become the cause of all "our" troubles. For example, faced with a lack of jobs, a whole neighborhood may succeed in pooling their individual frustrations by agreeing on a common enemy. "It's those . . . ! They're the cause of our troubles. They take all the jobs!" We feel better when we can identify a scapegoat and blame our troubles on an individual or a group.

Scapegoating can be seen in the racial tensions and gang warfare of some of America's cities. It was what drove the ethnic "cleansing" in the Baltics, and the slaughter of the Tutsi by the Hutu in Africa. The Holocaust in Nazi Germany remains one of history's most terrible tragedies of scapegoating.

Uniting around a cause of common dissatisfaction, we are able for a while to focus our misery outside of ourselves. Shifting our attention to another, then attacking this person, creates the illusion that we are dealing with our pain. We have a place to focus our anger so that we don't have to face up to its source within ourselves.

JESUS BECOMES A SCAPEGOAT

The society in which Jesus lived was under Roman occupation. Though the Jewish hierarchy resented Roman occupation, their power as the local government was sanctioned by the Romans and they benefited economically. So it was advantageous to them to keep society stable.

The religious authorities believed that God blessed the nation when the laws and taboos were observed, but cursed it when they were violated. Since the nation had lost its freedom, they concluded that it was because some sectors of society were violating the Law of Moses.

The religious rulers could be fairly sure they wouldn't be blamed for the state of things as long as there were disreputable people to point to as the cause of the nation's troubles. Society depended on such scapegoats for its stability.

When Jesus pointed out that God causes the sun to rise on both sinners and saints, and sends rain on those who do wrong as well as on those who do right, he was upsetting the foundational beliefs of Judean society. If the unclean couldn't be blamed for the state of things, who could?

Jesus recognized that we are all part of a shared life grounded in God. When you realize this, you see the other as part of yourself. Consequently, with Jesus all divisions among people were broken down. Refusing to join society in its scapegoating, he shared his life with those who were ostracized by the social system, withholding neither from beggars nor outcasts the love of the Christ. By including society's traditional scapegoats in his company, he put himself on a collision course with the system of taboos that categorized people as "clean" or "unclean."

As the price for being the loving person that he was, Jesus himself became a scapegoat. His crucifixion was the result of a life lived with compassion for people. The rulers justified executing him as "expedient" for the sake of preserving the nation.

JESUS RESPONDED WITH LOVE

Jesus didn't blame either those who crucified him or his disciples for deserting him. On the contrary, when he returned to the disciples after his resurrection, the first word out of his mouth was, "Peace!" Instead of reminding them that they deserted him, he showed them compassion. This reinforced for them the unconditional nature of how Jesus loved.

In place of scapegoating, Jesus retrains us in the Christ's way of love. Rejected, he didn't become obsessed with those who had rejected him. Remaining in his own quiet place, completely non-reactive, he invited the disciples to experience the peace that "surpasses all understanding" of the Sabbath rest.

24

REACH FOR
THE SKY

—

We live our whole lives under the shadow of death. This doesn't merely mean that we know we will die. It means that our dread of dying impedes the way we live. It causes us not to live fully.

Instead of relishing life as Jesus did, reaching for its fullness, we seek security above all else. It's as if material security could somehow hedge us in from having to face what looks to us like the ultimate loss—the loss of our life.

Functioning in a protective mode, we hang onto our lives "for dear life." But actually, our attempt to hold onto our lives proves to be a stranglehold. It causes us to settle for being only half alive. We never become people who reach for our potential and thereby touch our world with the gift of a life fully lived.

The curious thing about Jesus is that he had a wonderful sense of himself, yet he wasn't in any way self-absorbed. Because he didn't live under the shadow of death, he had no need to engage in private world-building. Though as a human being he was finite, all of his actions were ignited by the transforming power of the Infinite.

Free of the need to build up his own little world, Jesus could identify with the whole world. He didn't see himself as a citadel. He opened himself up to such a degree that he identified with the whole pulsating energy of the cosmos.

YOU ARE COSMIC IN SCOPE

The letter to the Hebrews says that by showing us death in a new light, Jesus is able to "free those who all their lives were held in slavery by the fear of death." Seeing how Jesus viewed death gives us a different perspective on our own death. This changes how we live.

Who we really are has until now been lost in self-isolation. To participate in the kingdom of heaven is to discover our identity as part of a universal oneness. Reconnecting with the infinite Presence at the heart of creation, we experience ourselves as connected to everyone and everything.

Realizing that we are not worlds unto ourselves, we no longer live in a manner that says, in effect, "To hell with everyone but me." We no longer regard our little neck of the woods as if it were everything. Instead of exhibiting a monumental indifference to others—ignoring the fact we are part of the human race, forgetting that we are part of the ecosphere as we poison the soil, air, and water that sustain us—we instead live in a manner that acknowledges our oneness.

Emerging from our isolation, we become alert to our importance to the whole. We awaken to the impact our lives have on the lives of others, as well as on our planet and its many life forms. The sense of well-being this brings us causes us to promote the well-being of everyone and everything else.

As Jesus increasingly experienced himself as one with God, he increasingly realized that he was one with all humankind and one with the universe. His consciousness, spilling over the boundaries of his temporary physical existence, stretched toward the infinite consciousness in which the entire creation is grounded.

In embracing a universal identity, Jesus pioneered the destiny of us all. For in our true identity, we are all part of an infinite presence. This identity is at once the most private and the most universal reality. It's an identity that, while uniquely personal, is ultimately cosmic. Through it, we are connected to lives everywhere at all times.

DEATH FOR JESUS WAS A BECOMING

Even as we grow physically only by giving up one stage of development for another—the womb for the cradle, the cradle for crawling, crawling for walking—so also we grow spiritually through a lifelong process of death and resurrection. We die to one level of existence to discover another. Undergoing repeated death and resurrection is how our cosmic self is hatched.

Jesus continually died to how he understood himself, so that his life was a progressive discovery of himself as a more complex, richer person than he had so far known himself to be. In each new crisis, he left behind something he had outgrown to embark on a new phase of growth that challenged him to become more fully himself. The comfort of a home, the support of his family, the safety of the quiet life of Nazareth were shed, as he chose instead the hazards of the open road, the hardship of no fixed abode, the constant demands of the crowds, and the risks that went with being a public figure of whom the authorities disapproved.

What propelled Jesus to Golgotha? He was convinced that his death was the culmination of all he was born to be. With each step of his life's journey, he had entered into an ever-expanding sense of himself. By the time he emerged from those final hours in the Garden of Gethsemane, his being was stretched as far as his mortality permitted.

As long as we are in mortal bodies, we are restricted to a three-dimensional existence. Space and time rule us. But what if our ultimate destiny is to continue to outgrow ourselves as we now experience ourselves? Our lives then become an adventure in a context that has no limits.

Because Jesus' whole life had been one of continually dying and being reborn, it made sense to see physical death as the climax of this human experience. As he approached the hill of Golgotha, he was ready for the dissolution of his body—ready to take on a new mode of being. By dying, he wasn't experiencing the loss of himself. He was becoming more than he had ever been.

THE EXPERIENCE OF RESURRECTION

To talk of the resurrection of Jesus causes many of us to imagine him "out there" somewhere, separate from us. This isn't at all what the gospel images of the resurrection point to.

Said Paul, "But we all, with unveiled face, beholding *as in a mirror the glory of the Lord,* are being transformed into the *same* image *from glory to glory.*" Through looking into the mirror of Jesus in glory, we see who we are in the process of becoming.

Scriptural imagery tells us we have been raised up "*together* with Christ." This reveals the magnificence of our own true being, which isn't individualistic but collective. The imagery depicts a future far greater than the survival of a host of private, individual souls. It's an image of a global, and ultimately cosmic, community in which unconditional love is our everyday currency.

During his lifetime, Jesus had to walk alone the path of realization of his true being. As more and more of his Christ self became visible, those who were close to him enjoyed the reflection of this in their own lives. They started to understand who they too really were and began to enjoy the fruits of this discovery in the form of increased joy and peace.

But, as mentioned before, the *fullness* of the divine glory wasn't accessible to Jesus' disciples while he was still on earth. As he told them on the eve of his crucifixion, the Comforter—which he called the spirit of truth, or authenticity—could only come among them if he himself left them.[23]

We have seen that Jesus' sudden arrest and execution left his followers devastated. We have also seen that as they found themselves beyond all their coping skills, stripped of any ability to help themselves, they became aware of the spiritual bedrock of their being, with which they had not been in touch until now. In a state of absolute crisis, they realized that they too were experiencing within themselves the same loving presence they had known in Jesus when he was among them.

In spite of the fact that their situation looked desperate, and their beloved Jesus was no longer physically with them, they continued to feel unbidden surges of love and peace and joy that they had only previously experienced in Jesus' presence. For the first time, they came to realize these beautiful states of being were actually coming from within them. Indeed, Jesus did not leave them comfortless. He had done his job magnificently. The disciples were experiencing their own resurrection. The glory of the divine essence within them was taking over their lives. Instead of being reflected, it was coming from their own center. Ah, the ecstasy!

But this experience of true self-love, joy, and peace was only a foretaste of what was about to occur in their lives.

A COMMUNITY IS BORN

The Christ spirit that had come alive *within* the disciples was increasingly experienced as a transforming power *among* them. The man who never stopped growing grew into a community. This is depicted in the story of the day of Pentecost, told in the book of Acts.

With the coming of the Comforter, or Counselor, the disciples entered into a communal expression of the Christ consciousness—something that Jesus himself never experienced while he was on earth, which is why he said on the eve of his death that we would enjoy a "greater" experience of God's power than he himself did.

The Pentecost story depicts a further stage in the disciples' evolution into a life lived from divine consciousness. People of all nations were gathered to celebrate the Jewish festival in Jerusalem. On the morning of the festival, the disciples were gathered in a private room in the city. Suddenly, a strong wind crashed open the doors of the room, and tongues of fire lighted on the heads of those present. The disciples then rushed out into the streets, where people of many different languages all heard them as if they were speaking in their own tongue.

This imagery is drawn from the Genesis story of the Tower of Babel. Until the building of the Tower, everyone spoke a single language across the whole face of the earth. As the story has it, God separated the people into nations by confusing their speech, so that they spoke different languages. With the coming of the Comforter, this division of the world's peoples is healed. A new humanity, united as if one single human being—the corporate Christ—comes into being.

In the words of the letter to the Colossians, we "put on the new man, who is renewed in knowledge according to the *image of Him who created him*, where there is neither Greek nor Jew, circumcised nor uncircumcised, barbarian, Scythian, slave nor free, but *Christ is all and in all*."

The Pentecost image of tongues of fire resting on the disciples' heads is drawn from Roman coins, in which a tongue of fire on the Caesar's head denoted his divinity. The imagery in Acts represents the universalizing of this divinity. Recognizing the Christ self within themselves, the disciples simultaneously recognized it within each other. Thus was born a community characterized by a sense of oneness, which resulted in an unconditional love for each other.

As the disciples experienced the powerful connection of oneness between them, so also their understanding of each other became deeper and richer. They found themselves spontaneously reaching out to each other, sharing their lives on every level, opening up to each other at the most profound depths. A true intimacy, in which they could be transparent with one another, characterized their relationships. The degree of love they felt for one another was such that they were ready to lay down their lives for each other if necessary.

To know the Christ nature is to be awakened to a deep caring that pours out of us as love and creates companionship. Life touches life with a new sense of wonder and excitement. In this community, love flows freely back and forth.

Life lived in the oneness of the divine takes some getting used to. Though it is our most natural state, we have long been alienated from ourselves and therefore from each other. Our daily journey is therefore one of learning how to actualize our loving center, by trusting that love, and nothing but love, is our true nature.

As this love grows within and among us, it ultimately bursts at the seams of our mortality. We experience ourselves outgrowing our ability to contain it in physical bodies. We feel ourselves becoming ecstatically and lovingly "larger than life."

This enables us to embrace the next stage in our journey—a further death and resurrection. The grave becomes to us what it was for Jesus—the shedding of our limitations. We are ready, with him, to experience in full the love that pulsates throughout the universe.

25

HOW DO YOU REMEMBER YOUR FORGOTTEN SELF?

—

As the disciples experienced a love that was off the human scale, they recognized that they were in touch with a kind of inner life that the rest of the world had yet to experience.

We don't get this vital sense of ourselves, which enables us to experience our connectedness to everyone and everything, from growing up. We don't get it from society, which does everything it can to crush it. So where does it come from?

AWAKENING TO DIVINE CONSCIOUSNESS

What the disciples clearly experienced dramatically transformed their lives in a way that eludes many of us. Most of us struggle with being able to live the beautiful kind of life Jesus lived. We long for it, hope it will be true of us someday, but experience only a limited expression of it. Why?

In chapter 7 we saw that the key to feeling good about ourselves lies in how we see ourselves. We have to believe in our worthiness in order to experience ourselves as worthy. The same is the case when it comes to manifesting our divine nature.

"He who believes in Me," Jesus said, "out of his heart will flow rivers of living water." If we don't experience the "rivers of living water," then it's because we don't truly believe.

To believe in Jesus is to allow him to become *the way you see your-self*. You trust that the divine nature in which he participated is also your true nature.

How does this work in everyday life?

Take guidance as an example. You are faced with a situation in which you don't know what to do. So you ask for guidance, as Jesus said you should. Well, do you receive the guidance you are seeking?

I know of countless people who seek God's guidance but who tell me that they don't seem to receive an answer. When it comes to making a decision, they experience more uncertainty than certainty.

This is why the New Testament letter of James instructs, "If any of you lacks wisdom, let him ask of God, who gives to all liberally and without reproach, and it will be given to him. But let him ask in faith, with no doubting, for he who doubts is like a wave of the sea driven and tossed by the wind."

If you ask, you will receive. So if you don't feel like you know what to do, it's not because the guidance isn't being given. It's that you don't trust what's coming to you. You are in the condition James describes as that of "a double-minded man, unstable in all his ways." You waffle, doubting yourself, instead of moving forward confidently.

To live from divine consciousness is to cease reacting emotionally and cease thinking your way through life. Instead, the insight you need "flows" from deep within. The key is learning to trust it.

TRUST YOUR INNER "KNOWING"

Jesus was an astute observer of the world around him. He paid attention to the lilies of the field, the birds of the air, the wheat fields, the sunshine and rainfall, and the naturalness of little children. He saw how spontaneously and easily everything happened, emerging out of a state of deep calm.

At times Jesus made a special effort to hike into the mountains or out into the desert. Away from the hustle and bustle of the crowds, he was more alive than ever to the infinite Presence that permeates everything.

Because Jesus was so attuned to this Presence, which he called "the Father," whenever he needed insight, it simply arose within him. He was so finely attuned to his divine center that he did nothing without hearing from it. Divine truth guided his every move.

The difference between Jesus and many of us is that he trusted the insights that welled up within him. He had absolutely no doubt that divine "knowing" was guiding him in everything. This is why he could say, "I *am* the way, the truth, and the life." He embodied the "isness" of God. In each moment, pure divine inspiration poured through him.

There simply is no other way to experience the infinite Presence, other than in the way Jesus experienced it. Consequently he could say, "No one comes to the Father except through Me."

There is nothing exclusive in this statement—no "in group," no "us and them." Rather, it's inclusive of *everyone.* Jesus' way of being is open to all of us. We can only experience the divine if we are willing to enter into the frame of mind that was his continual state. We must participate in the same divine nature that he participated in—a nature that the name Joshua symbolizes.[24]

YOU ARE GOD MADE FLESH

When you are in touch with your inner stillness, where the divine essence of your Christ self is vibrantly alive, the norms of family, culture, and society no longer define you.

If those around you say, "You can't believe that!" or "You can't do that!" you no longer conform to these worldly limitations. You don't buy into such an inhibited way of thinking. Instead, in the words of Paul to the people of Rome, you experience a "renewing of your mind" that enables you to "prove what is that good and acceptable and perfect will of God." In more modern language, you are guided by a deep "knowing" that never fails you.

This is the meaning of the incarnation. The divine essence of the universe is expressing itself through you. Only your inability to believe this restricts your experience of it. In Jesus its expression was unrestricted because he learned to trust it with his whole being.

As Jesus found himself spontaneously reaching out to the leper, the woman caught in adultery, the rejected prostitutes, and despised tax collectors, he recognized that love was his true nature. Instead of believing that he was defective, as society claimed, he saw that his loving actions flowed from who he really was. Contrary to all his conditioning, he owned his goodness. As he came into this realization, he practiced it until he fully embodied it.

Jesus had ears to hear and eyes to see the truth about his humanity. He recognized himself as the incarnation of evolving divinity.

How can you remember that you are the Christ self? Switch your focus from what society says about you to the truth within you. Take your eyes off your inadequacies and instead become aware of all the good that arises in you each and every day. Realize it's the Christ nature seeking to burst forth. Allow it to become your primary consciousness, which will change you "from glory to glory," as happened with Jesus.

In other words, to believe is to *own* your divine nature. You own your oneness with God, just as Jesus did. You recognize that everything emanates from the Creator—that your whole life is the product of divine love, which uses everything that happens to you to awaken you to your Christ self.

This fires you with a tremendous faith in life, ending all self-doubt. When you approach each day with this kind of faith, it's the end of all searching. The divine qualities you have sought automatically well up within you.

"DOING WHAT COMES NATURALLY"

"Love one another as I have loved you," Jesus told his disciples on the eve of his death. How many of us are able to love as Jesus did? Yet Jesus considered it not only *possible* for us to do so, but *mandatory*.

The expression "as I have loved you" is usually understood to mean that Jesus' love is a special kind of love, a supernatural type of love. Since we don't think of ourselves as having this kind of love, we can only hope and pray that God will someday grace us with it.

As rare as divine love is currently among humans, paradoxically this love is our natural state. It's because we focus on *asking* for this love, waiting for it to be given to us, that we generally find ourselves incapable of loving in this way. Instead, we need to believe that *we are* divine love and *behave as if it came naturally.*

Perhaps you don't think of divine love as natural. Selfishness, alienation, and strife may seem more natural. This is because often what we consider "natural" to the human species actually comes from a limited sense of ourselves ingrained through thousands of years of human conditioning. However, no amount of time or conditioning can erase our Christ nature.

As you reconnect with your forgotten self, you become free of all the limitations and defenses you picked up from society. When this happens, your *own* floodgates open, and you discover yourself as an inherently loving person. You then experience what Paul called the "fruit" of the Spirit.

Said Paul, "The fruit of the Spirit is love, joy, peace, longsuffering, kindness, goodness, faithfulness, gentleness, self control." The word "fruit" is illuminating. These characteristics aren't something we have to strive for, any more than a fruit tree has to try to put fruit on its branches. Fruit comes into being naturally. Similarly, the divine characteristics bubble up from our divine essence. All we have to do is recognize them and embrace them as *authentic expressions* of our own nature. Fleeting though they may be at first, we have to trust that they are evidence of who we really are.

Our spiritual practice, then, is to observe these states that arise in us—moments of exquisite peace, times when we feel ecstatic, occasions when we see a way to help one of our fellow humans and are moved to do so, feelings of appreciation and gratitude that well up within us and we simply can't hold back from expressing them. We observe, we embrace, and we own these as aspects of our Christ nature.

It's all a question of focus. Dwell on your inadequacies, and you will live inadequately. Live from faith in your Christ self, and you will express your divine nature. As Paul wrote to the Romans, the good news of the Christ "is the power of God to salvation for everyone who *believes.*" Wholeness, which is the essence of your Christ nature, emerges solely as the result of trust. Indeed, Paul added, "The right-eousness of God is revealed *from faith to faith.*" The journey begins with believing in your Christ self and continues through believing in your Christ self. Faith—trust—is all that's required.

You *already* are everything you long to be. You always have been. To the degree that you *believe* it, you will *be* it.

Scriptural References and Allusions to Scriptures

CHAPTER 1

Matt. 11:28–30	Come to Me, all you who labor and are heavy laden, and I will give you rest. Take My yoke upon you, and learn from Me, for I am gentle and lowly in heart, and you will find rest for your souls. For My yoke is easy and My burden is light
Heb. 11:13–14	These all died in faith, not having received the promises, but having seen them afar off were assured of them, embraced them and confessed that they were strangers and pilgrims on the earth. For those who say such things declare plainly that they seek a homeland
Eph. 2:6	And made us sit together in the heavenly places in Christ Jesus
Eph. 1:3	Who has blessed us with every spiritual blessing in the heavenly places in Christ
Matt. 1:21	And you shall call His name JESUS, for He will save His people from their sins
Heb. 4:3–10	There remains therefore a rest for the people of God
Jn. 18:36	My kingdom is not of this world
Acts 17:25	Since He gives to all life, breath, and all things
Acts 17:28	For in Him we live and move and have our being

Jn. 10:10   I have come that they may have life, and that they may have it more
                   abundantly

Jn. 11:26   Whoever lives and believes in Me shall never die

CHAPTER 2

Heb. 2:6   What is man that You are mindful of him?

Heb. 2:10   The captain of their salvation

Jn. 14:9.   He who has seen Me has seen the Father

Matt. 11:30   For My yoke is easy and My burden is light

Mk. 13:11   Do not worry about how or what you should speak. For it will be
                   given to you in that hour what you should speak; for it is not you
                   who speak, but the Spirit of your Father who speaks in you

Phil. 4:7   The peace of God, which surpasses all understanding

Jn. 15:11   These things I have spoken to you, that My joy may remain in you,
                   and that your joy may be full

CHAPTER 3

Mk. 1:15   The time is fulfilled and the kingdom of God is at hand

Matt. 24:26   Therefore if they say to you, "Look, He is in the desert!" do not go out

Lk. 17:21   The kingdom of God is within you

I Jn. 3:2   Beloved, now we are children of God; and it has not yet been
                   revealed what we shall be, but we know that when He is revealed,
                   we shall be like Him, for we shall see Him as He is

Matt. 13:33   The kingdom of heaven is like leaven, which a woman took and hid
                   in three measures of meal till it was all leavened

Eph. 2:6   And made us sit together in the heavenly places in Christ Jesus

Jn. 14:3   I will come again and receive you to Myself; that where am, there
                   you may be also

Jn. 3:3   Unless one is born again, he cannot see the kingdom of God

Col. 1:13   He has delivered us from the power of darkness and conveyed us into the kingdom of the Son of His love

Jn. 8:36	Therefore if the Son makes you free, you shall be free indeed
Jn. 15:15	No longer do I call you servants, for a servant does not know what his master is doing; but I have called you friends
Rom. 5:17	Those who receive abundance of grace and of the gift of righteousness will reign in life through the One, Jesus Christ
Matt. 6:10	Your kingdom come

CHAPTER 4

I Cor.15:22	As in Adam all die, even so in Christ all shall be made alive
Eph. 1:23	Which is His body, the fullness of Him who fills all in all
Eph. 2:18	To create in Himself one new man
Dan. 7:13	One like the Son of Man, coming with the clouds of heaven!
Dan. 7:27	Then the kingdom and dominion, and the greatness of the kingdom under the whole heaven, shall be given to the people, the saints of the Most High
I Cor. 15:45	"The first man Adam became a living being." The last Adam became a life-giving spirit
Jn. 3:16	For God so loved the world that He gave His only begotten Son
Heb. 1:3	The brightness of God's glory and the express image of His person
Col. 1:15	He is the image of the invisible God, the firstborn over all creation
Jn. 1:18	No one has seen God at any time. The only begotten Son, who is in the bosom of the Father, He has declared Him
Jn. 14:9	He who has seen Me has seen the Father
Jn. 8:12	I am the light of the world
Matt. 5:14	You are the light of the world
Gen. 1:27	Let Us make man in Our image, according to our likeness
Eph. 1:22–23	The church, which is His body, the fullness of Him who fills all in all
Rom. 8:29	For whom He foreknew, He also predestined to be conformed to

	the image of His Son, that He might be the firstborn among many brethren
Col. 2:10	And you are complete in Him
Rom. 8:22	For we know that the whole creation groans and labors with birth pangs until now
Rom. 8:20	The creation was subjected to futility, not willingly, but because of Him who subjected it in hope
Rom. 8:19	The creation eagerly waits for the revealing of the sons of God
I Cor. 6:17	He who is joined to the Lord is one spirit with him
Phil. 1:21	For to me, to live is Christ
Gal. 2:20	It is no longer I who live, but Christ lives in me
Col. 1:27	Christ in you, the hope of glory
Jn. 17:22	And the glory which You gave Me I have given them, that they may be one just as We are one
Jn. 17:21	As you, Father, are in me, and I in you; that they may be one in Us.
Jn. 17:23	I in them, and You in Me, that they may be perfect in one

CHAPTER 5

Jn. 10:34	Is it not written in your law, "I said, 'You are gods'?"
Rom. 3:23	All have sinned and fall short of the glory of God
I Cor. 10:31	Whether you eat or drink, or whatever you do, do all to the glory of God
Jn. 17:22	The glory which You gave Me I have given them, that they may be one just as We are one
Psa. 8:4	What is man that You are mindful of him, and the son of man that You visit him?
Heb. 2:7	Crowned with glory and honor
Rom. 14:23	Whatever is not from faith is sin
Jn. 14:28	My Father is greater than I

Heb. 2:10	Bringing many sons unto glory
Heb. 2:11	He is not ashamed to call them brethren
Heb. 10:5–6	Sacrifice and offering You did not desire. In burn offering and sacrifices for sin You had no pleasure

CHAPTER 6

Matt. 10:14	Let the little children come to Me, and do not forbid them; for of such is the kingdom of God
Mk. 7:21	For from within, out of the heart of men, proceed evil thoughts
Jer. 17:9	The heart is deceitful above all things, and desperately wicked

CHAPTER 7

Rom. 7:18–19	For I know that in me (that is, in my flesh) nothing good dwells; for to will is present with me, but how to perform what is good I do not find. For the good that I will to do, I do not do; but the evil I will not to do, that I practice
Eph. 5:29	For no one ever hated his own flesh, but nourishes and cherishes it
I Cor. 6:19	Or do you not know that your body is the temple of the Holy Spirit who is in you, whom you have from God, and you are not your own?
Rom. 8:7	Because the carnal mind is enmity against God
Rom. 7:17	But now, it is no longer I who do it, but sin that dwells in me
I Tim. 6:12	Fight the good fight of faith
Rom. 7:24	O wretched man that I am!
Rom. 8:25	I thank God—through Jesus Christ our Lord!
II Cor. 10:5	Bring every thought into captivity
Rom. 8:5	Live according to the spirit
Rom. 5:17	Reign in life
Rom. 6:11	Reckon yourselves to be dead indeed to sin

CHAPTER 8

I Cor. 2:11	No one knows the things of God except the Spirit of God
II Pet. 1:4	Partakers of the divine nature
Eph. 1:18	The eyes of your understanding being enlightened
Eph. 4:18	Having their understanding darkened, being alienated from the life of God, because of the ignorance that is in them, because of the blindness of their heart
Jn. 17:16	They are not of the world, just as I am not of the world

CHAPTER 9

Lk. 9:23	If anyone desires to come after Me, let him deny himself, and take up his cross daily, and follow me
Jn. 15:15	No longer do I call you servants, for a servant does not know what his master is doing; but I have called you friends
Jn. 15:12	This is My commandment, that you love one another as I have loved you
II Cor. 3:3	You are an epistle of Christ . . . written not with ink, but by the Spirit of the living God, not on tablets of stone but on tablets of flesh, that is, of the heart
Heb. 8:10	I will put My laws in their mind and write them on their hearts
Rom. 10:8	The word is near you, in your mouth and in your heart
Phil. 2:8	He humbled Himself and became obedient to the point of death
Jn. 10:18	No one takes it from Me, but I lay it down of Myself.
Matt. 26:39	If it is possible, let this cup pass from Me
Heb. 12:3	Who for the joy that was set before Him endured the cross, despising the shame

CHAPTER 10

Jn. 4:5–42	

CHAPTER 11

Jn. 15:7	Ask what you desire
Matt. 7:7	Ask, and it will be given you; seek, and you will find; knock, and it will be opened to you
Matt. 6:32	Your heavenly father knows you need all these things
Jn. 10:10	I have come that they may have life, and that they may have it more abundantly
Lk. 6:38	Give, and it will be given to you: good measure, pressed down, shaken together, and running over will be put into your bosom
Jn. 15:7	If you abide in Me, and My words abide in you, you will ask what you desire, and it shall be done for you
Lk. 2:41–50	"Did you not know that I must be about My Father's business?"

CHAPTER 12

Rom. 8:5	For those who live according to the flesh set their minds on the things of the flesh, but those who live according to the Spirit, the things of the Spirit
Titus 2:12	Ungodliness and worldly lusts
Jn. 3:16	That whoever believes in him should not perish
Jonah 2:6	The earth with its bars closed behind me forever; yet You have brought up my life from the pit
Jude 7	Suffering the vengeance of eternal fire
Matt. 10:24	It shall be more tolerable for the land of Sodom in the day of judgment than for you
Ezek. 16:55	When your sisters, Sodom and her daughters, return to their former state
Heb. 5:8–9	He learned obedience by the things which He suffered. And having been perfected, He became the author of eternal salvation to all who obey Him

CHAPTER 13

Jn. 7:15   How does this Man know letters, never having studied?

Lk. 9:58   Foxes have holes and birds of the air have nests, but the Son of
                  Man has nowhere to lay his head

Matt. 10:35–36   For I have come to 'set a man against his father, a daughter against
                  her mother, and a daughter-in-law against her mother-in-law'; and
                  'a man's enemies will be those of his own household'

Lk. 14:26   If anyone comes to Me and does not hate his father and mother,
                  wife and children, brothers and sisters, yes, and his own life also, he
                  cannot be My disciple

Lk. 14:16–24

Matt. 12:46–47   Who is My mother and who are My brothers?

Lk. 4:28–29   So all those in the synagogue, when they heard these things, were
                  filled with wrath, and rose up and thrust Him out of the city; and
                  they led Him to the brow of the hill on which their city was built,
                  that they might throw Him down over the cliff

Mk. 10:28   See, we have left all and followed You

Acts 2:44   Now all who believed were together, and had all things in common,
                  and sold their possessions and goods, and divided them among all,
                  as anyone had need

Acts 4:32   Neither did anyone say that any of the things he possessed was his
                  own, but they had all things in common

CHAPTER 14

Lk. 17:21   The kingdom of God is within you

CHAPTER 15

Mk. 1:15   Repent, and believe in the gospel

Lk. 24:47   Repentance and remission of sins should be preached in His name
                  to all nations

Lk. 5:20   Man, your sins are forgiven you

Lk. 5:23	Which is easier, to say, 'Your sins are forgiven you,' or to say, 'Rise up and walk?'
Jn. 8:36	Therefore if the Son makes you free, you shall be free indeed
Jn. 8:11	Go and sin no more
I Jn. 5:18	We know that whoever is born of God does not sin
I Jn. 3:6	Whoever abides in Him does not sin. Whoever sins has neither seen Him nor known Him
I Jn. 3:9	He cannot sin, because he has been born of God

CHAPTER 16

Lk. 7:34	For John the Baptist came neither eating bread nor drinking wine, and you say, 'He has a demon.' The Son of Man has come eating and drinking, and you say, 'Look, a glutton and a winebibber, a friend of tax collectors and sinners!'
Heb. 4:15	For we do not have a High Priest who cannot sympathize with our weaknesses, but was in all points tempted as we are, yet without sin
Gal. 2:20	I have been crucified with Christ; it is no longer I who live, but Christ lives in me
Matt. 18:3	Unless you are converted and become as little children, you will by no means enter the kingdom of heaven

CHAPTER 17

Matt. 16:22–23	Then Peter took Him aside and began to rebuke Him, saying, "Far be it from You, Lord; this shall not happen to You!" But He turned and said to Peter, "Get behind Me, Satan! You are an offense to Me, for you are not mindful of the things of God, but the things of men."
Lk. 22:42	Not My will, but Yours, be done
I Jn. 4:14	And we have seen and testify that the Father has sent the Son as savior of the world

CHAPTER 18

Heb. 9:22   Without shedding of blood there is no remission

I Jn. 4:18   There is no fear in love; but perfect love casts out fear, because fear involves torment

Rom. 3:23   For the wages of sin is death

Eph. 2:1   And you He made alive, who were dead in trespasses and sins

II Cor. 5:14   If One died for all, then all died

Rom. 5:9   Much more then, having now been justified by His blood, we shall be saved from wrath through Him ·

I Pet. 4:17   For the time has come for judgment to begin at the house of God

Lk. 15:11–32

Rom. 1:28   God gave them over to a debased mind

Ps. 139:7–8   Where can I go from Your Spirit? Or where can I flee from Your presence? If I ascend into heaven, You are there; if I make my bed in hell, behold, You are there

Rom. 5:8   But God demonstrates His own love toward us, in that while we were still sinners, Christ died for us

II Cor. 5:19   God was in Christ reconciling the world to Himself, not imputing their trespasses to them

CHAPTER 19

Isa. 53:5   And by His stripes we are healed

I Cor. 2:2   For I determined not to know anything among you except Jesus Christ and Him crucified

Ezek. 18:2   The fathers have eaten sour grapes, and the children's teeth are set on edge

II Cor. 5:14–15 For the love of Christ compels us, because we judge thus: that if One died for all, then all died; and He died for all, that those who live should live no longer for themselves, but for Him who died for them and rose again.

CHAPTER 20

Jn. 16:7	It is to your advantage that I go away; for if I do not go away, the Helper will not come to you; but if I depart, I will send Him to you

CHAPTER 21

Matt. 27:45	Now from the sixth hour until the ninth hour there was darkness over all the land
Matt. 27:51	The earth quaked and the rocks were split
II Cor. 5:14	If One died for all, then all died
II Cor. 5:17	Old things have passed away; behold, all things have become new
Jn. 14:2	In My Father's house are many mansions
Jn. 14:2–3	I go to prepare a place for you. And if I go and prepare a place for you, I will come again and receive you to Myself; that where I am, there you may be also
Jn. 2:16	Take these things away! Do not make My Father's house a house of merchandise!
Jn. 1:51	Hereafter you shall see heaven open, and the angels of God ascending and descending upon the Son of Man
Gen. 28:17	This is none other than the house of God, and this is the gate of heaven!
Gal. 4:19	My little children, for whom I labor in birth again until Christ is formed in you
Eph. 1:3	Who has blessed us with every spiritual blessing in the heavenly places in Christ
Phil. 2:10–11	That at the name of Jesus every knee should bow . . . and every tongue should confess that Jesus Christ is Lord
II Pet. 1:4	That through these you may be partakers of the divine nature
Rev. 11:15	The kingdoms of this world have become the kingdoms of our Lord and of His Christ
Rev. 5:5–6	Behold, the Lion of the tribe of Judah

Rev. 5:10	And have made us kings and priests to our God; and we shall reign on the earth
Matt. 20:27	And whoever desires to be first among you, let him be your slave
I Cor. 15:28	That God may be all in all

CHAPTER 22

Matt. 5:44	Love your enemies
Matt. 5:39	Whoever slaps you on the right cheek, turn the other to him also
II Cor. 5:16	Even though we have known Christ according to the flesh, yet now we know Him thus no longer

CHAPTER 23

Deut. 28:2	And all these blessings shall come upon you and overtake you
Matt. 5:45	He makes His sun rise on the evil and on the good, and sends rain on the just and the unjust
Jn. 11:50	Nor do you consider that it is expedient for us that one man should die for the people, and not that the whole nation should perish
Jn. 20:26	"Peace be to you!"
Phil. 4:7	The peace of God, which surpasses all understanding

CHAPTER 24

II Cor. 3:18	But we all, with unveiled face, beholding as in a mirror the glory of the Lord, are being transformed into the same image from glory to glory
I Cor. 15:28	That God may be all in all

CHAPTER 25

I Jn. 3:14	We know that we have passed from death to life, because we love the brethren

Jn. 7:38	He who believes in Me . . . out of his heart will flow rivers of living water
Jas. 1:5–8	If any of you lacks wisdom, let him ask of God, who gives to all liberally and without reproach, and it will be given to him. But let him ask in faith, with no doubting, for he who doubts is like a wave of the sea driven and tossed by the wind
Jn. 14:6	I am the way, the truth, and the life. No one comes to the Father except through Me
Rom. 12:2	Be transformed by the renewing of your mind, that you may prove what is that good and acceptable and perfect will of God
Jn. 15:12	Love one another as I have loved you
Gal. 5:22	The fruit of the Spirit is love, joy, peace, longsuffering, kindness, goodness, faithfulness, gentleness, self control
Rom. 1:16	For I am not ashamed of the gospel of Christ, for it is the power of God to salvation for everyone who believes
Rom. 1:17	The righteousness of God is revealed from faith to faith

Endnotes

1   For insight into the nature of the portraits of Jesus found in the gospels, see: Spong, John Shelby. *Liberating the Gospels: Reading the Bible with Jewish Eyes*. New York, NY: HarperCollins. 1996.

2   For this reason, the debate over whether God exists—whether you can "prove" there is a God scientifically—is futile. There isn't a being called God, separately identifiable from the creation. But the unfolding evolution of the universe happens within the infinite presence we call God.

3   Moore, Sebastian. *Let This Mind Be in You—The Quest for Identity through Oedipus to Christ*. New York, NY: Harper & Row. 1985. I am especially indebted to Sebastian for this insight, who first brought it to my awareness in *Let This Mind Be in You*, now out of print. Subsequently, we corresponded extensively on this theme, through which I gained many insights that are shared in this book.

4   "Beloved, now we are children of God; and it has not yet been revealed what we shall be, but we know that when He is revealed, we shall be like Him, for we shall see Him as He is," says I Jn. 3:2. The full revelation of the Christ involves all of us becoming the embodiment of God as Jesus was. Only when we are all like Jesus do we finally see the Christ in full glory.

5   Matt. 26:64 says, "Hereafter you will see the Son of Man sitting at the right hand of the Power, and coming on the clouds of heaven." Hereafter means "from now on," and refers to the time of Jesus' death and resurrection. Notice the sequence: the Son of Man sits at the right hand of power, and comes on the clouds of heaven. He doesn't come first, then reign. The kingdom of God began at the time of Jesus and involves a continuous coming that culminates in its full revelation. The "clouds of heaven"

involved in this coming are a symbol of the saints: "Since we are surrounded by a great cloud of witnesses" (Heb. 12:1). In I Thess. 4:16-17, the saints are described as being caught up into the clouds to meet the Lord in the air. The imagery points to the uniting of the heavenly and earthly realms, as who we are in our divine essence takes on flesh and becomes the embodiment of the Christ.

6   The expression "born again" has a dual meaning in Greek. It also means "born from above," speaking of the heavenly dimension. It is to become conscious of our divine nature.

7   Following the tradition of the King James Version, the New King James also uses language that isn't gender inclusive. However, the Greek word *anthropos* is inclusive, unlike the word *aner* which means "a male." It should more correctly be translated "human being."

8   The book of Daniel describes a vision in which "One like the Son of Man" is pictured seated at the right hand of God. The title "Son of Man" had a long history in Israel. It was first used almost a thousand years before the time of Jesus in psalms attributed to King David. Over the centuries, its meaning evolved. By the time the book of Daniel was written, it no longer meant simply a human being but had taken on divine attributes. From his heavenly throne, the Son of Man comes to earth in the clouds of heaven to replace the world's empires with the kingdom of God. When Daniel sees this Son of Man who has assumed world rule, he isn't simply an individual. The Son of Man comprises "the saints of the Most High." This is the Christ, the body of people who function as if they were a single human in the very image and likeness of God.

9   The expression "only begotten son" needs to be heard not in twenty-first century terms, but for what it meant to Greek-speaking people at the time of Jesus. Philo of Alexandria, a Jew who wrote in Greek at about the time of Jesus, spoke of "a human" arising out of God's own being. In Philo's understanding, this "human" is "begotten" of God, but he isn't an individual. He is all humans. When Philo spoke of the "begotten" Son of God, he was referring to the essence of humanity. For an understanding of Philo's thought in comparison with the Gospel of John, see: Waetjen, Herman C. *The Gospel of the Beloved Disciple*. New York, NY: T. & T. Clark. 2005.

10 This essence, which is God's nature, is referred to both in the Gospel of John and the writings of Philo as the *logos* (often translated the "word"). The Greek term logos retains its essential meaning in our English words "logic" and "ontological." It refers to the underlying order of the universe, an order reflected in the structure of language—hence its frequent translation as the "word." This underlying order, found in

nature and expressed through our use of words, is the image, or reflection, of God's essence. It is intrinsic to the being of God, not an afterthought. Thus the creation reveals the very nature of the Godhead (Rom. 1:20). As part of the evolving creation, Jesus, in whom the self-expression of God through the logos reaches its epitome, is the "express image" of God (Heb. 1:3). He is the measure of what all humans are in process of becoming (I Jn. 3:1-2). Hence we might think of the logos as the blueprint for what we are all becoming.

11 The entirety of Matthew chapter 12 upholds the dignity of human beings. We are more holy than any of the things we consider holy. Though evil may invade our lives, depicted as Beelzebub invading a house, it has no rightful place in us because our house—who we really are—is divine. Evil stems from not recognizing how magnificent we are. As long as we refuse to see our goodness—indeed, our Godness—we have no hope of experiencing forgiveness, for we blaspheme the very Spirit of God which is our essence when we imagine ourselves to be evil. How can we feel forgiven if we feel we are evil? This is to sin against the Holy Spirit—to resist our true nature. How we see ourselves determines the kind of life we live—a life manifesting the goodness of God, or a life manifesting evil.

12 Moore, Sebastian. *The Crucified Jesus Is No Stranger*. New York, NY: Crossroad. 1989. Also, Moore, Sebastian. *Let This Mind Be In You—The Quest for Identity through Oedipus to Christ*. New York, NY: Harper & Row. 1985.

13 Crossan, John Dominic. *Jesus: A Revolutionary Biography*. New York, NY: HarperCollins. 1994.

14 Malina, Bruce J. *The New Testament World, Insights from Cultural Anthropology*. Atlanta, GA: John Knox Press. 1981.

15 The NKJV uses the word "gospel." I have provided my own translation because the word gospel is archaic. Gospel simply means "good news."

16 Galatians 5:24 states, "And those who are Christ's have crucified the flesh with its passions and desires." The expression "the flesh" is not speaking of the physical body, but of our carnal thoughts and emotions, devoid of the direction of our spiritual center. Passion can be destructive or loving, as can so many of the body's appetites. Living "according to the Spirit" means we use our minds and bodies in a manner that's whole—nothing of who we really are is held back. We live passionately. Living "according to the flesh" means we function in a dysfunctional, destructive way, ignoring much of who we are.

17 Various terms are used throughout the New Testament to speak of the effect of Jesus' death. We have been bought with a price, redeemed with his blood, purchased with his own blood, ransomed. None of these expressions have anything to do with God needing to be appeased or any kind of debt having to be paid before God can forgive us.

God's love and forgiveness, overlooking all our sins, has never been withheld, never been in question. It is we who have been blind, gone astray, and become lost as to our true identity. We have sold ourselves to the limited view of ourselves the world confers on us. It is this that we are brought back from. We are redeemed from the way our minds have enslaved us in a world that knows nothing of the heavenly dimension of our being, our divine essence.

Jesus on the cross reveals that even when we murder the most innocent of beings, in whom God is enfleshed, we are totally forgiven, accepted and loved. Realizing this restores in us the ability to see ourselves through the loving eyes of God.

Our sins are said to be "remitted" through the propitiatory sacrifice of Jesus. It is not God who requires our sins to be remitted, or a propitiation, or expiation. It is we who require these things because we simply cannot accept how loved and lovable we are. We have to be convinced of our lovability, despite all we have done. This is what the death of Jesus accomplishes. It mirrors how we kill our true selves, and therefore each other—then says to us, "You are forgiven, because you don't know what you are doing."

Atonement is a making-at-one, which happens when we at last quit being down on ourselves as if we were no good and allow ourselves to be loved by God. It is we who need to be made aware of our oneness with God. God has never been anything but one with us.

18 This is the meaning of the statement that only by the "blood" of Jesus are we saved, or made whole. In killing Jesus, humanity commits the ultimate crime, and by means of this crime discovers how alienated each of us has been from our true self. Acceptance of ourselves leads to wholeness—salvation.

19 By touching the root of our pain, he breaks the cycle of humans being hurt and then hurting both themselves and others. Quoting Isaiah, the disciples said of Jesus, "By His stripes we are healed." The death of Jesus as victim is the only thing that can touch us at sufficient depth to heal us. As Paul explained, a victim's soul resonates with nothing "except Jesus Christ and Him crucified." Jesus on the cross exposes what has been done to you—and what, as a result, you do to yourself and to others. As a symbol of your true self, he shows you not only your self-crucifixion, but also your crucifixion of others.

20   A dominant image of Jesus in the gospels is that of a suffering servant, an image bor-
     rowed from the book of Isaiah. This has widely been interpreted to mean that Jesus
     endorsed suffering as a way of pleasing God. Self-flagellation has for 2,000 years been
     seen by many as a holy act. But the role of suffering servant wasn't forced on Jesus—it
     was chosen. He took it upon himself in order to show once and for all that our spiritual
     bedrock state can never be that of victim, for our divine essence is nothing but love.

21   Thus Paul could write to the Corinthians concerning Jesus' effect on his life, "For *the
     love of Christ compels us*, because we judge thus: that if One died for all, then all died;
     and He died for all, that those who live should live no longer for themselves, but for
     Him who died for them and rose again."

22   Mark, and later Matthew and Luke, described a time of great trouble that would
     accompany the second coming. It's important not to confuse this actual time of trou-
     ble, which occurred in history, with the apocalyptic language used to describe the end
     of the world.
         The time of trouble these three gospels describe wasn't a global event but local-
     ized. Matthew makes it clear that it was to affect only the land of Judea (Matt. 24:15-
     22). People living in Judea should flee to the mountains. If you lived outside Judea,
     you should stay outside. People should also pray that this didn't occur in winter or
     on the Sabbath—which would make no sense were this a global event, since when it's
     winter in one hemisphere, it's summer in another. The statement that "no flesh"
     would survive unless this time of trouble were shortened refers to Jews in Judea, not
     throughout the world.
         When you read Luke's account of this prophecy, its local character becomes even
     clearer. Luke makes it plain that the Gentile nations were not affected. Wrath would
     be upon "this people," the people of Judea, not upon the whole world. It involved the
     desolation of Jerusalem by armies, which came true when Rome sacked the city (Lk.
     21:20-24). All of this would be fulfilled within a generation of when Jesus spoke these
     words (Matt. 24:34). A generation is forty years. Jesus began his ministry about the
     year 30. The desolation of Jerusalem came in the year 70.
         Before this event, the Good News would be preached to all nations. Paul said this
     had been accomplished under his ministry. It had been "preached to every creature
     under heaven," he attested (Col. 1:23).
         Immediately after the great tribulation, people would notice the sign of the son of
     man in the heavens and see him coming in the clouds (Matt. 24:30). We have seen
     that the second coming is an increasing awareness of the Christ self in humans. It
     isn't an instantaneous event, but occurs over a long period of time—though the
     earliest gospel writers do not seem to have fully understood this.

The Gospel of John was the last of the four gospels to be written, coming about a quarter of a century after Mark, the first to be written. The Gospel of John says nothing about a time of trouble. Neither does it use apocalyptic language. Why?

One reason John doesn't mention what the other gospels call a "great tribulation" is that it had passed. But it's also clear that John's understanding had evolved beyond that of the first writers.

Paul said that as far as prophecies are concerned, he knew only in part, saw only in a limited way, and this would mean that sometimes prophecies would fail (I Cor. 13:8-9). He was pointing to the fact that the followers of Jesus grew in their understanding. In the years between when Mark wrote and the last gospel appeared, they came to see the second coming differently. Their attention switched from expecting a supernatural intervention, to realizing that the collective body that makes up the new humanity, the Christ, was increasingly appearing on earth, spreading like leaven in flour. It's a kingdom that is descending from the "heavens," from the inner dimension of spirit into the external realm of the world. Hence John, writing the last of the four gospels, found no need to introduce apocalyptic imagery. His focus switched to living in Christ consciousness in everyday situations, which results in a life of loving service.

23 The word Comforter, sometimes translated as Counselor, means one who comes alongside—like someone who advocates for you in court. I like the term presence, since to "receive" the Holy Spirit is to become aware of God's continuous presence both within us and in every aspect of our lives.

24 This is why the author of the book of Acts could say that "there is no other name under heaven given among men whereby we must be saved" (Acts 4:12). Claiming the name of Jesus doesn't bring wholeness to our lives. Participating in his nature does.

n)

NAMASTE PUBLISHING

Our Publishing Mission is to make available healing and
transformational publications that acknowledge, celebrate, and
encourage readers to live from their true essence and thereby
come to remember Who They Really Are.

*

Namaste Publishing
P.O. Box 62084
Vancouver, British Columbia V6J 4A3
Canada
www.namastepublishing.com
Email: namaste@telus.net
Tel: 604-224-3179
Fax: 604-224-3354

To place an order, see www.namastepublishing.com, or
Email: namasteproductions@shaw.ca

To schedule David Ord for a teaching or speaking event,
Email: namasteteachings@telus.net

To receive the full benefit of books from Namaste Publishing, we
invite you to read our daily blog: "He said ... She said ..."

We also invite you to sign up for our free Email Newsletter, in
which we bring you articles by our staff writers, book and movie
reviews, frequent free downloads from our authors, and informa-
tion about forthcoming publications.

You may sign up for both the BLOG and the NEWSLETTER by
going to our home page: www.namastepublishing.com